Home/Land/Security

Home/Land/Security

What We Learn about Arab Communities from Action-Adventure Films

Karin Gwinn Wilkins

LEXINGTON BOOKS

A division of
ROWMAN & LITTLEFIELD PUBLISHERS, INC.
Lanham • Boulder • New York • Toronto • Plymouth, UK

LEXINGTON BOOKS

A division of Rowman & Littlefield Publishers, Inc.
A wholly owned subsidary of The Rowman & Littlefield Publishing Group, Inc.
4501 Forbes Boulevard, Suite 200
Lanham, MD 20706

Estover Road
Plymouth PL6 7PY
United Kingdom

British Library Cataloguing in Publication Information Available

Library of Congress Cataloging-in-Publication Data

Wilkins, Karin Gwinn, 1962–
  Home/land/security: what we learn about Arab communities from action-
adventure films / Karin Gwinn Wilkins.
     p. cm.
  Includes bibliographical references and index.
  ISBN-13: 978-0-7391-2785-8 (cloth: alk. paper)
  ISBN-10: 0-7391-2785-3 (cloth: alk. paper)
  ISBN-13: 978-0-7391-3214-2 (e-book)
  ISBN-10: 0-7391-3214-8 (e-book)
  1. Arabs in motion pictures. 2. Action and adventure films—United States—
History and criticism. I. Title.
  PN1995.9.A68W55 2009
  791.43'652927—dc22

                                                              2008038380

Printed in the United States of America

♾™ The paper used in this publication meets the minimum requirements of
American National Standard for Information Sciences—Permanence of Paper for
Printed Library Materials, ANSI/NISO Z39.48–1992.

For my Dad
Donald Monroe Wilkins

Contents

Acknowledgments

This project represents my attempt to address critical concerns with the nature and extent of prejudice in U.S. society. I appreciate the resources and privileges that have allowed me to speak on these issues.

There are many more people who have inspired and supported this work than I can name. I am quite grateful for the social, intellectual, and financial support generously shared with me throughout the course of this project. The research itself was financed through a University of Texas Special Research Grant, as well as through research internships and assistantships sponsored through the University of Texas and the Department of Radio-Television-Film. This department, along with the Center for Middle Eastern Studies, generously funded our Workshop on Re-visioning Arab Communities in US Media, bringing together media professionals with academics and advocates to consider the merits and limitations of various strategies to attempt to improve mediated representations.

Many friends and colleagues have provided a strong and compassionate intellectual community that has nurtured this effort. I particularly want to express my appreciation to Dana Cloud for her constant encouragement, diligent reading, and thoughtful suggestions, as well as to Bob Jensen for helping me to find a useful structure and for naming this project. For their leadership and encouragement in pursuing these topics even when potentially controversial, I appreciatively recognize John Downing, Tom Schatz, and Sharon Strover. For their insightful ideas and seasoned support, I also want to thank Doug Boyd, Hemant Shah, Jack Shaheen, Joe Straubhaar, and Lawrence Wright. Martha Diase and Elissa Nelson provided constructive skills and critical contributions in their work throughout the

ix

research process. I am indebted as well to the professional contributions of Susan Dirks, Gloria Holder, Chris Lucas, Holly Custard, Assem Nasr, Young-Gil Chae, Tom Maguire, Becky Lentz, and Joslyn Massad.

I am particularly grateful for the steadfast support of my family and friends. For their love and affection during the course of this project, I thank wholeheartedly Alexander Monroe Siegenthaler, Katherine Grace Siegenthaler, Karel Grace Knudsen Wilkins, Susan Harnden, Richard Lewis and Arturo Carlos Madrid.

I gratefully acknowledge receipt of a University Co-operative Society Subvention Grant awarded by The University of Texas at Austin for publication costs.

1

Introduction

Terrorism defines our political landscape, structuring public policies as well as justifying military intervention. The terrorist attacks of 9/11 devastated the United States, not only in terms of the immediate destruction of many lives, but also in terms of the enduring effects on the American psyche. The United States has used the threat of foreign violence to the national homeland to justify stringent domestic and exploitive foreign policies, leading to more human loss in Afghanistan, Iraq, and other territories, as well as provoking racial profiling and harassment of Arab, Muslim, and South Asian communities in the United States. The narrative of terrorism and its consequences is stimulated and reinforced through suspenseful mediated tales chronicling the power of good to vanquish evil. The intersections between our imagined concerns articulated in these narratives blend unceremoniously with projected fears in our lived experiences. Fear experienced in our daily lives must account for a broader set of circumstances triggered by terrorism, encompassing fear of travel, of others, and of discrimination.

The constructed narratives of terrorism in popular culture suggest the ways in which dominant ideologies are structuring our interpretations of global conditions in which events occur, our senses of fear and blame for conflict, as well as our desire for heroic conquest as resolution. At essence the representation of power through mediated texts implicates a particular political perspective, reinscribing the dominance of U.S. forces, all the more pertinent when dealing with issues of global events and national security.

In post-9/11 United States, the importance of securing the national homeland against global threats has become a relatively uncontested

1

foundational trope in our political rhetoric. These concerns have been institutionalized in the United States through the establishment and work of the Department of Homeland Security, as well as through domestic policies such as the Patriot Act, and foreign policies such as military intervention in Afghanistan and Iraq. These policies and procedures rely on normative acquiescence to the idea that the people and the nation must be protected. Reigning political forces have been able to exploit this interest in security in order to advance a variety of agendas, justifying intensified control over citizens and technologies in the name of the public interest. Resistance to the particulars of these policies, such as antiwar protests and civil rights litigation, mark these as complex concerns competing with a variety of other core values in U.S. society, such as the right to privacy and the sanctity of human life; yet even these struggles against dominant U.S. policies have difficulty confronting this fundamental concern with security.

In order to sustain a hegemonic interest in using issues of national security to justify political strategies, the broader ideological discourse must be in accordance with the particular positions asserted. Mediated discourse of terrorism, in news as well as popular culture, accentuates a foreboding of potential threats to the principles and people we hold dear. In the context of post-9/11 United States, the discourse of terrorism takes on particular significance as a way of asserting political control over individual lives, building on a sense of threat to the nation. This sense of nation builds on this sociopolitical construction imagined and reinforced through mediated texts (Anderson 1983; Appadurai 1996). These threats become manifest in fears of "others" outside of the territorially bound, culturally identified nation. As a way of enforcing actions to deal with these threats, those exemplifying the ideals of the nation are positioned as powerful in their capability and morally righteous in their determination to use force or whatever means necessary to annihilate enemies. Our collective sense of threat, fear, and resolution finds inspiration in the dominant narratives in our media.

This work focuses on what we learn from the genre of action-adventure film about our nation within a global sphere, about Arab communities, and about fear and security. Because focusing on a single text cannot capture the social fabric of our daily experience, in this research project I attempt to address the broader media environment in which we live. In particular, I focus on the genre of action-adventure film and consequences of its pervasive and persuasive narratives of good and evil. Such stories use identification with a conquering hero to cultivate fear of "others" who, in the narratives, pose a threat to the security and sanctity of the homeland. This particular genre allows this study to mediate between the potential effects of viewing media more broadly and the reception of particular texts, offering a vehicle for dialogue on global space as well as race, ethnicity, nationality, and other instances of privilege and oppression.

So what might we learn from action-adventure film? Through the characterization of villains and the suspenseful plots of terrorism, we learn about security. Through the mapping of cultural groups in relation to territorial settings, we learn about land. Through the illustration of heroes, we learn about the idealization of home. These narratives of security and the homeland articulate particular lessons about the United States, Arab communities, and the Middle East. This education, though, is neither simplistic nor monolithic, but interpreted within particular social and political contexts.

Recognizing the importance of these contexts, my research explores how focus groups identifying with Arab American communities, in contrast to other U.S.-based communities, differ in their reading of action-adventure film. Specifically, intermediary research questions concern how viewers interpret villains as manifestations of threats to security; film settings in relation to fear within global space and the Middle East; and heroes engaged in conquering evil. Focusing on audience interpretation, this study addresses a neglected empirical link between well-documented problematic media representations and Arab American experiences with discrimination and oppression, as well as others' knowledge of and attitude toward Arab communities and the Middle Eastern region.

Referencing the vast literature on mediated representations of Arab communities, we see that one of the most persistent tropes filtering portraits of Arab characters in the genre of action-adventure is the narrative of terrorism. Mediated narratives of terrorism follow consistent patterns, whether across news or fictional genres, increasingly more blurred than distinct. Nacos's (1994) analysis of terrorist event representations in the 1980s through early 1990s suggests that media coverage tends to focus on hostages and their relatives, for example. Clearly positioned within a commercial media industry, sensationalist attention to drama and suspense, combined with filtering complex situations into simplistic stories of good and evil, are evident in descriptions of events within the genre, the settings within global space, and the central characters, delineating villains from heroes.[1]

In terms of the events depicted, the nature of the violence presented tends to be devoid of historical or political context (Muscati 2002; Wilkins and Downing 2002). As Karim (2000) explains, not attending to the underlying politics of the issues means that media audiences may be left unable to comprehend the reasons leading to acts of violence. This context is critical in attempting to understand historical relations of power, such as those enacted within and across Islam and the West (Tehranian 2000). The portrayal of Islam is particularly problematic given the unduly simplistic plots characteristic of terrorism narratives. Said (1997) and others (Adnan

1989; Baker 2003; Elayan 2005; Karim 2000; Mowlana 1995) point to the particular difficulty the U.S. media have in offering a more comprehensive portrayal of Islam, defined by some influential voices as a central threat (Salame, 1993). Karim's work explores the Orientalist framing of terrorism, through the use of language, visual imagery, and formats, as accentuating the identity and practices of Islam. Critics have singled out films such as *True Lies, Executive Decision,* and *The Siege* for equating Islam with terrorism (Ahmed 2002). Although the issues pertaining to the definitions and practices of Islam and Arab cultural communities are distinct, their fusion in mediated discourse in the United States transgresses the parameters of these stereotypes (Naber 2000).

Critics also point out the broad brushstrokes used to paint monolithic, unrealistic, and misleading images of Middle Eastern settings (Deep 2002; Muscati 2002). The region tends to be constructed as a violent land, rooted in a traditional culture opposed to civilization and democracy (Karim 2000). The diversity of Islam (Tehranian 2000) similarly becomes lost in these mystical settings. Khatib's (2004) analysis of the spatial representation in Hollywood films, in contrast to Egyptian films, demonstrates the tendency of U.S. media to portray domestic settings as green and orderly in juxtaposition with a disorderly, crowded, and dirty urban setting or a barren, wild desert landscape connoting the Middle East. Eisele (2002) argues for a genre specifically addressing films set in the Middle East, encompassing subgenres relating to Arabian nights narratives, sheik characters, foreign legion, foreign intrigue, and terrorists, differing in their potential degree of identification with the Arab "other." The terrorist subgenre particularly builds on Orientalist motifs in travel guides, literature, and other print representing Arabs as backward, hostile villains. While Turkey, Iran, and Israel do get included in Middle Eastern settings within the terrorist subgenre, typically the central setting of violence becomes codified as Arab (Eisele 2002).

In addition to projected settings, main characters central to the terrorism narrative exemplify idealized constructions of heroes and villains, indicating particular power dynamics resonant within broader social power structures. Arab and Muslim communities are more likely to be characterized in the role of villain than in the role of hero. There are numerous studies describing the limited and negative portrayals of Arabs and Muslims in U.S. news media (Kamalipour 1995; Sheikh et al. 1995; Suleiman 1988; Wolfsfeld 1997). Studies of Palestinian and Israeli conflicts (First 2002; Noakes and Wilkins, 2002; Zelizer, Park, and Gudelunas 2002) point to the consistent characterization of Palestinians as terrorists and of Arab society as inherently violent.[2] Visual representations in news accentuate differences, projecting Arabs and Muslims as menacingly violent, as traditional, and as religiously fanatic (McConnell 2003; Steet 2000; Wilkins

1995). Arab communities are described in terms emphasizing disorder and tradition, in contrast to the projected agency, civility, and modernity of Western societies (Sensoy 2004). The "demonization" of Arabs predates 9/11, though over time it has eclipsed the Communist enemy prevalent fifty years ago (Marrison 2004).

These characterizations resonate with those found in television and film as well (Ghareeb 1983; Kamalipour 1995; Shaheen 1984, 1997, 2000a, 2006). Shaheen's classic texts assessing the portrayals of Arabs in television (1984) and in film (2001) document the demonization and dehumanization of these characters in fictive narratives. Arabs tend to be positioned as antithetical to projected Western values (Alaswad 2000), portrayed as irrational and uncivilized, emphasizing loud dialogues in Arabic (Deep 2002). Even when historically inaccurate, such as in the film *Gladiator* about ancient Rome, Arabic-speaking men appear as villains (Shaheen 2000b). Elayan's (2005) analysis of Hollywood films prior to 9/11 establishes the preponderance of negative portrayals of Arab characters as historically conditioned rather than recently launched.

The countercharacter reinforcing this construction of power dynamics is exemplified by the typically White, male, American hero. In order to demonstrate the projected inferiority of "othered" characters in villain or victim roles, whether African American (Mask 2004), Asian (Shah 2003), or Arab (Shaheen 2004), White Americans are cast as the heroic characters who correctly recognize and solve problems. As Shome (1996) explains, "the white savior" fights oppression, particularly in "third world" countries through his superiority and paternal righteousness. Action-adventure heroes, even if varying accents and appearances somewhat, typically are White, heterosexual men (Holmlund 2004). This White "center" becomes positioned then as a cultural norm, obscuring the visibility then of this as a dominant positioning.[3]

Ethnicity, nationality, religious affiliation, gender, and other indications of power become aligned with clearly identifiable heroes and villains, in particular settings, within the genre of action-adventure. This genre is selected for analysis given its acknowledged narrative structure, in which villains tend to be positioned as foreign, ethnic, and racial "others," particularly Arab and Muslim (Marchetti 1989; Shaheen 2001). Genre here is understood in terms of its sociological connotations, bridging the assumptions and expectations producers and audiences bring to repeated conventions of the text (Neale 1995; Negus 1998; Schatz 1995). Action-adventure as a specific genre becomes noted for its "spectacular physical action," including physical fighting and grand explosions situated in a "white / male/ hero/ American capitalist dreamscape" in which settings are either historical or exotic (Neal 2004, 71–74). Krämer (1999) describes action-adventure films as inspiring audiences to feel "the fear and suffering of the protagonists in the early stages of the narrative and later into their triumphant violence and its attendant satisfaction (which may verge on outright sadistic pleasure at seeing the bad guys suffer and die)" (111). Neale establishes this genre as "linked with colonialism, imperialism and racism, as well as with traditional ideals of masculinity" (2004, 76).

The perceived constraints of the genre are recognized in public discourse when particular films are subject to critique. Film reviews and news coverage of protests over *The Siege*, for example, demonstrate how the projected limitations of the action-adventure genre are used to justify problematic portrayals in response to concerns raised by advocacy groups (Hall 2001; Wilkins and Downing 2002). These excuses combine with discussions of the film's purported realistic nature and the film professionals' intentions. However, there remains the concerns raised regarding the potential long-term consequences of these stereotypically defined heroic and villainous characters, Arab communities, and foreign landscapes.

MEDIATED ORIENTALISM

Grounded in a framework of mediated Orientalism, this work positions the production and consequences of mediated texts within positions of privilege and prejudice particular to post-9/11 U.S. society. Orientalism (Said 1978) operates as a dominant framework, building on historical experiences of political and economic imperialism, through which Western institutions exploit territories ascribed to a region entitled the "Middle East," the very naming of which exposes a particular perspective not grounded in indigenous conceptualizations. The process of imposing political and economic domination necessitates an attempt to control an ideological landscape, creating a context in which that very act of domination seems justified and understood, not questioned but instead part and parcel of conventional wisdom. Ideological justifications for domination then become manifest in the discourse of Western institutions, including media organizations as well as universities, corporations, military units, and other agencies. The media industry, along with these other organizations, portrays the region and its associated communities in particular ways that reinforce a justification and explanation for Western domination.

Media discourse accentuating violent and fearful acts without attention to the complexity of political and historical issues is not separate from but indeed rooted in historical relations of power (Karim 2000). In this discourse, Islam has emerged as the primary "other," replacing communism, as a key condition in opposition to Western values (Baker 2003; Karim 2000; Marrison 2004). The homogenization of Arab communities and conflation with other Middle Eastern as well as Islamic communities can be seen as part of a process benefiting dominant groups, such that subordinate groups can be cast more easily as inferior masses in mediated news as well as popular culture.

Mediated texts need to be understood within the professional, organizational, political, and economic contexts in which people create these cultural products. Hamada (2001) connects these problematic representations to the producers of this content, demonstrating the tendency of these professionals to view Arab communities as promoting fundamentalism and terrorism while resisting Western values and gender equality. The production of mediated texts operates within this broader framework in which Orientalist ideologies persist in political as well as cultural agencies, structured through the economic imperatives of the media industry.

Mediated images of terrorism justify and inspire approaches to U.S. foreign policy. Media, government, and military institutions construct versions of political problems and global conditions through an Orientalist lens. Muscati (2002) argues that mediated portrayals of war, through the dehumanization of Arabs and Muslims accentuating their threat as "other," inspired public support for U.S. intervention in the Gulf War and in Iraq. Apart from this indirect link between mediated images and foreign policy through expressed public opinion, direct connections between popular culture production and foreign policy are evident.

Toby Miller (2007) and others refer to the historical working relationship between the politicians in Washington, D.C., and the cultural producers in Hollywood as "Washwood." For example, White House staff met with Hollywood directors, actors, and writers to discern shared interests in promoting shared ideological values in the post-9/11 world. Lewis, Maxwell, and Miller (2002) explain this connection in terms of the film industry's reliance, in part, on government aid to subsidize production and distribution, reconciled with the political administration's aim to promote a convincing public relations campaign. American and European cinema are able to perpetuate "colonial discourse," advancing their political agendas, in part through their "monopolistic control of film distribution and exhibition in much of Asia, Africa, and the Americas" (Shohat and Stam 1994, 103). The hegemony of "global Hollywood" builds on a strong connection with Washington politicians, advancing national ideological interests while strengthening global commercial profits (Miller Govil, McMurria, Maxwell, and Wang 2005; Prince 1992).

An interview with Jack Valenti (2002), former president and CEO of the Motion Picture Association of America, clarifies the intersection between Hollywood film industry interests and U.S. foreign policy objectives. He explained his interest in securing explicit support from the film industry to explain to the world "not just about how wonderful America is, but about things that America has done. We have clothed and fed and sheltered millions and millions around the world without asking for anything in return." In his articulations of U.S. enemies, Valenti further reinforced the link between the narratives of action-adventure and U.S. foreign policy:

> Well, we know one thing about the culture of some of these people we are dealing with. They only understand force. To back down in the face of someone who has hit your family is to show weakness and softness. If you are not willing to avenge the death of your own, then you are nothing. So, this is a war where you cannot be hesitant. Benevolence is a word that must be struck from our vocabulary in this war. To talk about peace and forgiveness at such a time as this would provoke waves of derisive laughter in those caves in Afghanistan. (2002, 70–71)

While Valenti was not advocating directly for the use of more Arab or Muslim terrorist villains in Hollywood films, his statements did imply that it was necessary to project these images specifically in Arabic-speaking communities, intimating that these are the places from where most of the terrorist threats are likely to originate.

The intent to spin foreign policies and interventions is clearly demonstrated in the articulation of a new "paradigm" of public diplomacy as well as the professional public relations campaigns designed to project and limit news attention around the world to the administration's perspective, as in the case of U.S. bombing in Afghanistan (Solomon 2001). Recognizing the "image problems" of the United States in other countries, a Council on Foreign Relations task force suggests integrating a formally structured organization devoted to public diplomacy into the consideration and implementation of foreign policies (Peterson 2002). Interest in attracting non-U.S.-based communities to American cultural values, even if not advocating specific policies, is grounded in a long history of U.S. radio broadcasting to other countries, through the Voice of America and many other services. More recently, the Middle East Radio Network has been established, including Radio Sawa (in 2002 as part of the post-9/11 response) along with a website, to promote American cultural values through music and news programming to Arab audiences. Similarly, the satellite television station Alhurra, supported by U.S. government financing, broadcasts news and other programs in the Arab world. As former U.S. ambassador Rugh (2004) explains, given that "9/11 terrorists used our planes to kill our people, we should be able to use Arab media to inform and educate Arab audiences."

U.S. response to terrorism needs to be positioned within this broader context of political history and ideological currents. Quick to blame and slow to comprehend, U.S. discourse on terrorist events tends to attribute responsibility to Arab and Muslim communities, even before evidence clearly delineates such, as in the case of the 1995 Oklahoma City bombing. Global as well as domestic terrorist anti-U.S. attacks are initiated by a variety of groups and many regions, yet the proportionately fewer events associated with Middle Eastern groups gain considerably more attention. U.S. State Department records of political violence in 2002, for example, document 26 percent of all anti-U.S. incidents in the Near Eastern region (corresponding with the "Middle Eastern" region), compared with 11 percent in the Western Hemisphere, 30 percent in Europe, 26 percent in East Asia, and the remaining 7 percent distributed across Africa and South Asia (U.S. Department of State 2003); records from the year 2000 demonstrate similar trends, though with proportionately even fewer cases in the Near East and South Asia. This focus indicates the strength of an Orientalist discourse that perpetuates and legitimates the construction of Arabs and Muslims as culturally predisposed to terrorism.

While Orientalism refers to global contexts in which Western institutions impose their will on Middle Eastern communities, the broader process of hegemonic domination applies broadly to other sets of circumstances leading to oppression globally as well as locally. Communities within the United States also face discrimination, particularly when faced with the normative Anglo, Christian, heterosexual, male center of power. Yet the hegemonic process is far from stagnant or monolithic. Media have the potential to serve as a contested site through which groups struggle to assert particular visions, framing events, communities, problems, and potential solutions. The underlying concern is that the pervasiveness of mediated stereotypes contributes to a climate of prejudice, possible yet difficult to challenge.

PRIVILEGE AND PREJUDICE

Mediated characterizations of racial and ethnic groups reflect their hierarchical positions within broader social structures in ways that facilitate the hegemonic justification of those who wield privilege against those who face prejudice. While there is extensive literature demonstrating the limited characterization of Arab communities, of Islam, and of the Middle East, in popular as well as news narratives, we know much less about the consequences of these media portrayals.

An underlying concern with this project is the extent to which media contribute to the ongoing discrimination against particular communities. As Downing and Husband (2005) explain, this discrimination results from prejudice, or preconceived conceptions of other groups, sustained through mediated stereotypes. Representation of the "other" becomes manifest in these "precise and material" mediated stereotypes (Rameriz-Berg 2002, 38). Operating more as a source of socialization than of information, Dahlgren (1982) finds, Western audiences of television news are less likely to remember the details of news about other countries but instead have stereotypes of the third world as "other" reinforced. Media contribute to and sustain our construction of social reality through repetitive patterns in narratives over time (Morgan and Shanahan 1997).

Prejudice targeting groups along racial lines essentializes diverse groups with complicated histories into excessively simplified categories. The idea of race represents political hierarchies and processes rather than clear biological determination (Kromidas 2004). Recognizing "race" as a social construction signifying political and social conflict, ascribed in particular historical contexts for political purposes, some advocate instead referencing "ethnicity," encapsulating more potentially situational and hybrid conditions (Downing and Husband 2005; Omi and Winant 1994). However, not only are these terms complex in their histories and applications in current political discourse (Omi and Winant point out how theories of ethnicity tend to blame the victim and concentrate on differences across rather than within groups), but their ambivalent relevance to Arab American communities further accentuates their problematic character.

While self-identification as Arab American may be more concrete, attempts to define Arab culture in racial or ethnic terms become much more amorphous. Naber argues that Arab Americans are "simultaneously racialized as whites and as non-whites" (2000, 37). According to official U.S. institutions, Arab Americans are defined as White, or Caucasian, yet within normative climates their experiences may be more resonant with others in marginal, non-White communities. Biologically, Arab Americans are not easily classified into one racial or ethnic category, but instead may constitute this identity based on cultural, ancestral, and linguistic conditions, at times structured for political purposes (David 2007; Naber 2000). When distinguished in terms of a shared Arabic heritage and language, even these characteristics belie the complexity of this group, given that most speak English at home or quite well (75 percent), and many of the Arab dialects are not easily understood across groups. Further, Arab Americans include diverse religious affiliations, cultural backgrounds, physical appearances, and experiences of oppression (David 2007). The diversity within this group may be quite far ranging, yet the dominant normative categorization into one uniform collective, irrespective of socioeconomic, religious, and other key distinctions, demonstrates the vulnerability of this community particularly post-9/11.

The broader issue of institutional and normative prejudice holds merit, though, regardless of the difficulty in applying clear boundaries around the race or ethnicity of particular communities. What matters here is how the practices and structures of dominant institutions become routinized in ways that disregard critical issues of difference. As race becomes a profound yet largely unquestioned way in which we come to understand our world through essentialist categories, structures of domination are perpetuated (Omi and Winant 1994). Individual experiences need to be recognized as reflective and constitutive of broader institutional and social conditions with political ramifications. Institutional racism does not require malevolent intent for individuals to operate, but instead becomes manifest in the ways certain groups become privileged over others in their access to social, cultural, political, and financial capital.

Nor does normative racism require the conscious ill will of individuals to succeed in creating climates of oppression. The centrality of privilege is such that groups in power become entrenched in a normative center, where it is not just that others are at a disadvantage but those within the center hold clear advantages (Shome 1996). Jensen (2005) details how this dynamic grounds the foundation of privileges held by White constituents in U.S. society.

How we learn to disentangle complicated sets of racial and ethnic hierarchies builds on these normative assumptions learned through "discursive repertoires" (Frankenberg 2004, 344) in our social experience as well as through mediated texts. As Grey (2001) explains, White viewers are assumed to be a central subject within the commercial television industry, such that other viewers then gain visibility through their status as political subjects. Embedded within mediated texts are ideological frameworks that may reinforce existing power relations across groups, but may also have the potential to shift attention and framing of particular groups and issues. These texts, in their manifestation of power relationships within society, also need to be understood within the organizational contexts and political economic conditions that structure production and distribution. In terms of understanding the long-term consequences of normative racism perpetuated through media, more attention to media publics is warranted, particularly how dominant groups appropriate meaning in ways that facilitate White privilege (Downing and Husband 2005). It is the long-term accumulation of mediated representations of racial inequality that need to be recognized as contributing toward "devastating and dangerous situations"(Downing and Husband 2005, 117–18).

The problems of inequality need to be understood not merely in terms of social and cultural differences, but even more in terms of consequences to political status and economic welfare. Articulating how this inequality across groups becomes reinforced through media, contributing to broader dynamics, is part of this project. The construction of conflict accentuates this inequality by tending to privilege communities with power in positions of conquest against other more marginalized communities as perpetrators and as victims of violence. Ascribing an urgent need to particular situations, along with an incapacitated and therefore grateful victim, works to justify U.S. intervention. This characterization of privilege and prejudice contributes to cultural memory.

MEDIATED MEMORY

In this study, I explore audience perceptions of action-adventure film as a way of exploring the role of projected narratives and stereotypes in our cultural memory. Mediated Orientalism becomes immersed within our cultural understanding of the world as perspectives resonant with this dominant framework are more assumed than questioned in mediated texts. Collective memory of historical events, along with assumptions about the causes and consequences of these events, build from authoritative perspectives projected through mediated narratives.

Cultural memory, while grounded in mediated perspectives, is also predicated on personal identification with various communities. As Shah explains in his discussion of Asian culture, identities demarcate differences, perpetuated through the production and distribution of symbolic codes within media. Previous research has established the role of prejudice in coloring cultural memory of mediated images (Rockler 2002). For example, an experiment asking Caucasian viewers to recall African American and Caucasian criminal suspects, having seen edited newscasts, demonstrates that over time these viewers were more likely to mis-identify the race of the criminal suspects (Oliver 1999). Other experiments with Caucasian subjects confirm this pattern: Gorham's experimental research (2006) with White viewers of constructed television news demonstrates that discussions of White suspects were more concrete while discussions of Black suspects were more abstract, and that these differences in the nature of talk were more prominent among heavy news viewers and readers; similarly, Johnson, Adams, Hall, and Ashburn's (1997) experiment displaying White and Black perpetrators of violent acts demonstrated how Black male violence was more likely to be attributed to dispositional rather than situational conditions. Gender differences also contribute to divergent reactions to action-adventure texts, as established in an experimental study of the effects of humor channeled through heroes and villains on audience distress (King 2000). Oliver (1999) concludes that while her experiment was able to document some prevailing effects of racist attitudes, future studies should attempt to address existing media portrayals, rather than those displayed through experimental conditions.

Research clearly documents the limited and negative characterization of Arab communities in Western media, yet we know much less about potential empirical consequences (Majaj 2003; Wilkins and Downing 2002). Research on U.S. public opinion, as articulated in surveys and polls, demonstrates a consistent anti-Arab sentiment (Daniel 1995; Shaheen 1997, 2000a; Slade 1980). Sergent, Woods, and Sedlacek (1992) adapted a situational scale of prejudice to assess views of Arab assimilation, concluding that the studied college freshmen were more likely to feel threatened and suspicious of Arabs than of others joining their social groups. Respondents' concerns with being on a plane with Arabs or child custody cases involving Arab fathers were related loosely, though not empirically, to media stereotypes.

Few studies, however, do connect anti-Arab attitudes empirically to media consumption. An exception, Salazar's (2004) experimental research assessed attitudes toward Arabs following the viewing of films edited to highlight negative portrayals (such as scenes from *True Lies* and *Rules of Engagement*) versus those with more positive images (such as *Three Kings*). Subsequent prejudices were related to the types of images viewed, as well as their overall film-viewing habits, their experience in Arab countries, and having Arab friends.

Other studies of prejudicial attitudes toward Arab and Muslim communities presuppose media stereotypes as contributing toward a broader climate, rather than including media channels and texts explicitly into their research designs. Abouchedid and Nasser's (2006) survey of Floridian college students establishes that prejudicial attitudes toward Arab communities are predicated on racial background (Arab Americans being less negatively inclined than White, Hispanic, African Americans, Asians, and others) as well as knowledge of the Arab world. Although they assume explicitly that media represent problematic stereotypes that contribute toward problematic public opinion as well as foreign policy, empirical work is confined to examining differences across knowledge and racial identity. In her study of fourth graders' constructions of race in a Brooklyn, New York City, public school, Kromida concludes that "shared experiences of oppression do not *necessarily* build unity" (2004, 30). Concerned with the problematic stereotypes of Arab and Muslim cultures perpetuating fear in a post-9/11 climate, she illustrates how these mostly African American, Hispanic, and Asian children integrate diverse groups, including people from Pakistan, India, Afghanistan, Palestinian territories and others, into a racialized, xenophobic configuration of terrorists. She demonstrates how these perceptions filter into broader fears of foreign, dark-skinned "ugly" others they want to "kill," translating into explicit prejudice against Muslim and some South Asian students within the classroom. More research exploring an empirical relationship between mediated images and attitudes would contribute substantially to these discussions of race and ethnicity within cultural memory.

The underlying approach to this research is positioned between more conventional audience reception studies, in which audiences are viewed as actively interpreting media texts in ways consistent with prior conceptualizations, and more traditional media effects studies, in which audiences are viewed as passively responding to dominant characterizations in media texts. Following the direction engaged by Cloud (1992) and Condit (1989), this analysis recognizes the potential limits of seeing texts as fully polysemic, but instead proposes them as ambivalent (Cloud 1992) or as polyvalent (Condit 1989), particularly in relation to controversial issues, such as racial identity and abortion, as addressed in their respective analyses. Particularly useful in their work, as illustrative of broader subsequent trends in the field since, is the positioning of cultural texts and reception within particular historical moments (Hall 1985), demonstrating the way in which particular meanings serve the interests of dominant groups. In this study, understanding the role of Arab American communities within post-9/11 United States represents a critical historical juncture.

ARAB AMERICAN COMMUNITY AND IDENTITY

The construction of Arab American identity builds on a complex set of cultural foundations and political associations. Institutional articulations of Arab American identity focus on issues of ancestry. Estimates of this population in the United States vary widely, from a more conservative accounting based on the 2000 U.S. census, at 1.2 million, to 3 to 5 million speculated by national advocacy groups as well as commercial marketing firms (Allied Media 2006; Arab American Institute 2005; Brittingham and de la Cruz 2005; Salaita 2005). This discrepancy is based on the ways that individuals are asked to identify themselves in different research instruments. Official census counts miss constituents when classifying Palestinians as refugees or as Israelis when attributing background to the last country of residence, for example. The concern with enumerating ethnic groups, including Hispanics as well as Arab Americans, has fostered intensive political debate on how to conduct a valid accounting of identity in the U.S. census.

About one-fifth of Arab Americans, when identifying their ancestry for the U.S. census, articulate an overarching "Arab" category. Those who identify with a specific Arab nation affiliate with Lebanese (28 percent), Egyptian (14.5 percent), Syrian (8.9 percent), Palestinian (7.3 percent), Jordanian (4.2 percent), Moroccan (3.6 percent), and Iraqi (3.5 percent) heritage (de la Cruz and Brittingham 2003). Nearly half (46 percent) of this group was born in the United States. Among those not born in the United States, nearly half have arrived since 1990. Migration from this region in the late 1800s brought mostly Christians from Syria and Lebanon into the United States, but more stringent policies curbed immigration from 1925 until 1948. Post World War II, wealthy Palestinian families fled their homes in 1948, followed by others from Egypt, Syria, and Iraq over the next few decades (Naber 2000).

Separate from these institutional calculations, the assertion of Arab American identity tends to follow a more political stance than a monolithic cultural foundation. Not all who might be considered Arab American by official or other designations identify themselves as such. Particularly in a currently hostile climate, some see identifying as Arab to be at odds with an American allegiance (David 2007). Others prefer to identify through their families' national backgrounds, such as Lebanese, or through their religious affiliations, such as Christian or Muslim (Ajrouch and Jamal 2007; Salaita 2005). In a study of people of Arab descent in the Detroit area, those who do not tend to think "Arab American" describes them are more likely to categorize themselves as "White" (Ajrouch and Jamal 2007). While some may downplay their Arab heritage, others strongly assert an Arab American identity as a way to enhance credibility with U.S. audiences and politicians based on shared citizenship, as well as to transcend Arab national boundaries toward creating a panethnic identity (Witteborn 2007).

Given the extensive diversity within this community, it may be that political consciousness and engagement are more likely to define this group (David 2007). This identity takes on special meaning in the post-9/11 climate, but can be traced to political consciousness emerging from the 1967 Arab-Israeli war, when Americans of Arab descent experienced the consequences of a strong pro-Israeli foreign policy and of concomitant mediated denigrations of Arab cultures. Political activism grew in this post-1967 period with the emergence of organizations and advocacy groups devoted to the interests of Arab American communities (David 2007; Suleiman 2007).

The assertion of an Arab American identity relies on a political consciousness of experience within the United States as well as of geopolitical events in the Middle East (David 2007; Naber 2006; Salaita 2005). Aboul-Ela suggests that this very "dissident relationship to United States foreign policy in the Middle East is foundational to the experience of many Arab Americans and to a potential sense of Arab American community" (2006, 15). This political identity emerges in response to U.S. foreign policy that is perceived to be supportive of Israel as well as prejudicial to Arab cultures (Marshall and Read 2003). Recognition of shared patterns of discrimination and oppression, inspiring political engagement designed to improve political as well as media representation, can lead to community activism (David 2007). This political engagement may facilitate group membership for those who speak Arabic less well or who do not have identifiable Arab names or strong family ties to the region (David 2007).

Seeing Arab American identity as constitutive of community built on shared experiences of oppression and political engagement builds on an idealized sense of gemeinschaft, in which people feel solidarity within a collective that transcends individual interests. The notion of community may belie a hollow signification, as in a projected international community in which a "Muslim other" poses a threat (Semati 2008), or in contrast, it may offer a way of situating group identity based on perceived collective interest and experience of marginalization.[4]

This marginalization may be manifest in different ways, and not entirely in terms of economic opportunities. Although a relatively small group in relation to other defined communities within the United States (about 3 percent of immigrants, according to Allied Media, 2006), this group can be described as more educated and wealthier than most other American immigrant communities. El-Badry's (1994) description of the demographic characteristics of the Arab American community as younger, more educated, more affluent, and more likely to own a business pertains to more recent conditions as well. The commercial marketing firm Allied Media (2006) describes this group as "loyal, young, educated and affluent."

These descriptors seem to indicate a potentially attractive market niche, particularly given the media consumption patterns of young, urban professionals with disposable income. Compared to other groups in the United States, Arab Americans are more likely to fall within the twenty to forty-nine age group (31 percent, compared to 22 percent). This community also tends to be concentrated in selected cities and states (de la Cruz and Brittingham 2003). About two-thirds live in ten states, mostly in California, New York, and Michigan (Arab American Institute Foundation 2006). The mostly popular residential areas for this group include Los Angeles, Detroit, New York, northeastern New Jersey, Chicago, and Washington, D.C.

Within predominantly urban settings, Arab Americans tend to be more educated, more employed, and wealthier than other groups. Almost half (41 percent) of Arab Americans have at least a BA degree, compared with 24 percent in the general population. The proportion of those sixteen and older employed (80 percent) exceeded the national average (60 percent), according to 1990 statistics. This group is proportionately more likely to work in sales, as entrepreneurs, and to own businesses.

More recent estimates (Brittingham and de la Cruz 2005) of median household income show Arab Americans ($52,300) exceeding the national average ($50,000); this figure is more accentuated when dividing this by individual incomes of men (Arab men at $41,7000 compared with the national average of $37,100) and women (Arab women at $31,800 compared with the national average of $27,200). One caveat, though: while the median incomes of Arab Americans exceed those of the national average, this group is also more likely to be characterized in poverty conditions (17 percent) than the national average (12 percent), thus suggesting real disparities in terms of wealth within this community. In cities where Arab Americans are most concentrated, their median income is higher than others: for example, in the DC/MD/VA area, 1990 median household income estimates distinguish Arab Americans at $53,577 compared with $46,884, with similar trends in other cities such as Boston and the Bergen-Passaic and Los Angeles-Long Beach areas.

In terms of the economic conditions of the industry, the marketing potential of reaching Arab Americans is lost. If the logic of market economics does not explain narrow, negative characterizations of Arab communities, then what might? The problem lies not within the confines of the market system, but instead within the broader political-economic context of the United States and its relationship to the Arab region. The interests of an American elite endure, perpetuating hegemonic contexts in which long-term economic benefits are closely integrated with the political and cultural ideologies that structure relations between the United States and constructed Orientalist communities.

Within this Orientalist discourse, the diversity within the Arab American community remains obscure in U.S. media (Naber 2000). The conflation across Arab, Muslim, and Middle Eastern communities means that critical differences are buried, losing sight of Christian Arabs and non-Arab Middle Easterners. Arab Americans are hardly a homogenous group, differing dramatically not only in terms of origin, religious affiliation (roughly half identify as Muslim and half as Christian), and appearance, but also in terms of political beliefs (EPIC/MRI 2005). While most may share a concern with Palestinian issues, opinions on possible solutions to the Palestinian problems, as well as U.S. intervention in Iraq, differ greatly. Political affiliations distribute across Democratic (51 percent), Republican (27 percent), and other groups.

While the diversity within the group is lost in favor of a more generalized monolith, media coverage also does little in terms of highlighting violence and harassment against Arab Americans. In one critical illustration raised by constituents in this community, the murder of the American-Arab Anti-Discrimination Committee (ADC) regional director Alex Odeh received little attention in the U.S. mainstream media (Naber 2000).

Thoroughly saturated within the media environment, Arab Americans still recognize the problems with visible representation of their own and other communities. This community comprises avid fans of television and the Internet (75 percent have access), compared with many other groups.

Yet when asked how they thought Arabs were portrayed in television and film (EPIC/MRI 2005), most recognized largely negative characterizations (74 percent, with 18 percent undecided and 8 percent positive). When informants were requested to specify which outlets were the most negative, the most frequent responses included Fox News (24 percent), news in general (12 percent), and films in general (9 percent). Films specified in their open-ended answers include *The Siege, True Lies, Executive Decision, Die Hard, Rules of Engagement,* and *Air Force One.*

Hollywood films, along with television, have served as critical foci for groups struggling to resist dominant characterizations (Downing and Beltran 2002; Montgomery 1989; Pérez 1985; Shah 2003; Shankman 1978). Two central organizations protesting Arab and Muslim representation in U.S. media include the American-Arab Anti-Discrimination Committee (ADC) and the Council on American-Islamic Relations (CAIR). These groups have been actively challenging media characterizations (Shaheen 1997), documenting both media frames and Arab American experiences of harassment, discrimination, and hate crimes (ADC 2003). ADC and CAIR, along with other advocacy organizations, actively protested the problematic representations of Muslim and Arab characters in *The Siege,* promoting a discernible shift in public discourse on these issues (Wilkins and Downing 2001). As Arab Americans move from less visible to more "glaringly conspicuous" roles in post-9/11 United States (Salaita 2005, 149), concerns with stereotyping and discrimination are further heightened.

Observers of U.S. media and culture suggest that there has been a shift over time: prior to 9/11, Arab communities within the United States tended to be characterized as invisible and marginal. Naber's (2000) term "ambiguous insiders" aptly captured the "invisibility" of Arab immigrants into U.S. culture. She attributes this in part to institutional structures, such as those classifying Arab descendants in "multiple and conflicting categories" (38), and in part to the complex and shifting labels used within Arab American communities. While Naber advocates an internally driven and strategic quest for visibility, in recent years this group has come more into focus in ways that are not always welcome. Racial profiling and institutional surveillance, as well as normative climates of accepted discrimination and harassment, have accentuated a vulnerability accompanying this visibility.

Although the concern that U.S. news media and popular culture offer limited and negative representations of Arab communities is not new, this issue has become even more compelling given the increasingly hostile climate in which Arab Americans live. This climate is grounded in normative as well as institutional prejudice. Since 9/11, Arab Americans have witnessed an acceleration of incidents of harassment, discrimination, and violence (ADC 2003; Salaita 2005). Naber's (2006) ethnographic research confirms many accounts of the daily harassment experienced by Arab Americans in public spaces, as well as an "internment of psyche" in response to state surveillance.

In this post-9/11 climate, U.S. president Bush's War on Terror "over there" has become manifest in racism "over here" (Naber 2006). Institutionalized racism emerges as more and more Arabs and Muslims are questioned by state authorities and experience the consequences of racial profiling (Ahmad 2002; Akram 2002; Ali 2007; Amnesty International 2007). Previously established as a successful community of Arab American immigrants, the Arab Detroit area became the first city subjugated to the interrogations of a local Homeland Security office (Howell and Shryock 2003). The imperative patriotism described by Salaita (2005) has suppressed dissent of U.S. foreign policy as unpatriotic, as well as curtailed financial, political, and cultural ties to Arab countries as implying support of terrorist activities (Howell and Shryock 2003).

Some claim that since 9/11 there has been more interest in public discourse to help explain the nuances of Arab (and Muslim by popular conflation of these distinct groups) culture to mainstream Americans (Salaita 2005), through a variety of educational and mediated venues. Overall, however, mainstream media appear to be more resistant than conducive to these educational overtures.

To address these concerns, I consider how power and oppression, through the lens of home, land, and security, become articulated through mediated experiences, particularly within the context of action-adventure film. Audience reception of this genre is engaged through comparative analyses in an attempt to understand how Arab Americans experience these texts in relation to other U.S.-based communities (Hanania 1998).

RESEARCH APPROACH

My research explores how Arab American audiences differ from other U.S.-based communities in their interpretations and experiences as inscribed through dialogue inspired by discussions of action-adventure film. This study builds on an interdisciplinary approach calling for a variety of methodological techniques to help us explore how action and interpretation enable and constrain social and cultural structures. Specifically, my intermediary research questions concern how viewers interpret villains as manifestations of threats to security; film settings in relation to fear within global space and the Middle East; and heroes engaged in conquering evil.

In order to contrast perspectives raised in dialogue about action-adventure film, I conducted focus group research with Arab American and other U.S.-based groups. This process involved a purposive selection of invited participants who were solicited through university student groups at a large research university in the southern midwestern region of the United States. Given the limitations of this sampling procedure, generalizations across communities, places, and historical contexts are not appropriate.

A total of sixteen focus groups, comprising sixty-one individuals, were interviewed, half devoted to Arab American and half to other constituents. Two mechanisms were used for forming focus groups: first, a small group technique emerging in audience reception studies (thirty-three people in eight groups); and second, a more conventional focus group technique grounded in social science techniques (twenty-eight people in eight groups). Some of the central contact students were asked to form a small group for focus group study: this "small group selection" process, used in other audience reception studies reviewed in the literature, allows the formation of groups of people who are already familiar with each other, thus encouraging more frank and open discussions. Some degree of homogeneity within these groups may make potentially sensitive issues, such as those dealing with race and prejudice, more palatable. However, this technique does not always result in homogenous groupings: in another study a Caucasian girlfriend participated in a group with African American constituents (Rockler 2002). Similarly, focus groups in this research at times comprised a mix of informants.

In order to address potential methodological questions concerning the nature of these discussions, eight groups were formed through this small group technique, in which a central participant selected the other members of the group, while another eight groups were formed through more conventional focus group techniques, in which the researcher determined the composition of each group. Across these sixteen groups, half targeted Arab American participants (twenty-five focus group participants), four through small group and another four through focus group techniques. The remaining eight discussion groups were composed of informants from a variety of other ethnic backgrounds (thirty-six participants). Those focus groups that are not designed around attracting Arab American participants are referred to throughout the text as "other" focus groups (explicitly and intentionally shifting the focus from those typically designated as "other" when deviating from the normative center).

Focus group informants first completed an introductory survey and then participated in open-ended discussions. Surveys assessed extent of film viewing in general as well as action-adventure in particular; attitudes toward specific and typical film narratives and characters; self-identification in terms of race and ethnicity; and other demographic factors pertaining to gender, age, and socioeconomic class. This instrument offered a way to open conversation, by asking participants to begin thinking about their experiences watching action-adventure films.

Focus group discussions began with discussions of this genre of film, encouraging people to discuss the narratives and settings of particular films, and then to consider the race, ethnicity, nationality, religion, and gender of heroes and villains within these structures. In addition, informants described typical and ideal settings, heroes, and villains, as well as their experiences and attitudes concerning foreign travel, personal and national security, global events, and terrorism.

Focus group interviews lasted between one and two hours and were audiotaped and transcribed. Survey data were kept separately from focus group data in order to ensure the anonymity and confidentiality of each source. All participants were informed that the statements they made as part of the focus group discussions were confidential, and their survey responses anonymous. Each participant signed her or his consent to this clearly voluntary process. This process reflected standard procedures in accordance with the University Internal Review Board procedures and received approval from this group prior to research implementation. Research informants were awarded free movie tickets at a local movie theater in appreciation of their participation.[5]

Transcripts accorded to collective discussions comprise the focus group data analyzed, while open-ended responses as well as numerically coded close-ended responses constitute survey data analyzed. I analyzed these numerical survey data through SPSS (Statistical Package for the Social Sciences). Open-ended answers in these surveys were coded inductively toward categories that could contribute to SPSS analyses as well as inform interpretive patterns of responses.

Through these analyses I contrast dialogues across Arab-American and other groups, following a critical realist approach (Deacon, Pickering, Golding, and Murdock 1999) in which audiences are understood as both actively engaged in the construction of their social reality and constrained by structural conditions, such as social norms, economic conditions, policies, in a dynamic hegemonic system that enables resistance as well as dominance. By studying lived engagement with media through the genre of action-adventure film, these analyses address issues of race and ethnicity in relation to clearly defined roles, such as heroes and villains.

Research Informants

Research informants participating in these focus groups were relatively evenly divided across gender, with just over half (53 percent) being female. This group had a median age of twenty-one, encompassing mostly juniors (25 percent), seniors (23 percent), and graduate students (23 percent).

Most of these students were studying in the College of Communication (27 percent) or Liberal Arts (32 percent).

Two-thirds described their national identity as American (66 percent), with the rest identifying Arab (16 percent) or other (18 percent) domains. Although almost a third claimed no religion, others identified Christian (34 percent), Muslim (20 percent), Jewish (5 percent) and other affiliations. The open-ended question on racial/ethnic identity resulted in 36 percent claiming Caucasian, 24 percent Arab, 15 percent Asian, 9 percent Latino, and 2 percent African American. Note though that within the Arab American community there is some tension surrounding the point of whether to identify as Caucasian, Arab, or "other." Most of these informants had parents born in the United States. (41 percent fathers and 55 percent mothers). About 30 percent had fathers and 22 percent had mothers born in the Middle East. Other regions include Latin America (7–8 percent fathers and mothers), Asia (15 percent fathers and mothers), and other areas.

These broad demographics differed across the two different types of focus groups, half devoted to Arab American and half to others. Although all of the participants in the Arab American groups noted that they were U.S. citizens, only half (52 percent) identified their national identity as primarily American, with a third (36 percent) as "Arab," and the remaining as something else. The other groups identified themselves mostly as American in national identity (75 percent) and in terms of citizenship (89 percent). Their self-identified ethnic identities demonstrated a complexity of terms and interests: within the Arab American groups, most identified themselves as Arab (54 percent), though many wrote more lengthy descriptions of their identities (21 percent), or spoke of themselves as Asian (17 percent) or Caucasian (8 percent). The other groups were more mixed, divided among Caucasian (54 percent), Asian (14 percent), Latino (14 percent), African American (3 percent), Arab (6 percent), and others (9 percent). The Arab American groups were also more likely to have Muslim (44 percent compared with 3 percent), though fewer Christian (24 percent compared with 42 percent) participants. Other groups were more likely to have informants not want to identify a religious orientation (39 percent compared with 24 percent) or have those articulating "other" affiliations (11 percent compared with 4 percent). The proportion of Jewish informants did not differ greatly across groups (4–6 percent).

Experience with Action-Adventure

In this section, I explore research informants' engagement with action-adventure film. Specifically, intensive fans are contrasted with others, within Arab American and other focus groups, in terms of their active viewing and enjoyment of these films.

Arab American groups were much less likely than those in the other groups to enjoy or identify with the genre of action-adventure films. In a scale combining relative exposure and enjoyment, participants' answers to a number of questions were combined, including whether an action-adventure film was viewed in the previous month, how many action-adventure films on a provided list had been seen, and level of enjoyment of the genre (alpha = 0.71; eigenvalue = 1.9 predicting 63 percent of the variance). Almost double (64 percent) the percentage of other group participants watched extensively and reported enjoying this genre, becoming intensive fans; many fewer (36 percent) of the Arab American participants reported similar affinities (gamma = 0.52).

Across the two groups media consumption differed, with Arab American groups consuming slightly less television (1.5 hours in one day on average compared with 1.8 hours), but demonstrably fewer films (an average of 4.8 films in last month compared with 6.4, and circling on average 19 films on the provided list compared with about 23). Groups held similar preferences to most genres, although Arab American groups watched fewer action-adventure television programs (none, actually) than their counterparts (8 percent) in the week prior to their interview; less difference was found in terms of film preference, however.

Both sets of focus groups revered the suspenseful nature and special effects used in the genre. These themes resonated throughout discussions, exemplified by comments such as: "I go to these movies to see what cool things they will do with their vehicles, things that blow up" from an Arab American group and "good action scenes. When you see an action movie you kind of just suspend disbelief for awhile" from one of the other groups. While participants in both sets of groups seemed to share an interest in some of the defining features of the genre, their critiques diverged in critical ways.

WHAT WE LEARN ABOUT HOME/LAND/SECURITY THROUGH ACTION-ADVENTURE FILM

This work interrogates the ways in which political power permeates dialogue about action-adventure film, demonstrating how mediated Orientalism becomes manifest in the articulated discourse of these viewers. In the next chapter, I consider how issues of security, particularly in terms of fearing the threats personified by villains, surface in these discussions. Villains tend to be characterized as somehow less than human without particular personality or identity, particularly when non-White, Muslim foreigners. For some, these villainous characters are realistic given global conditions; for others, they represent simplistic, limited stereotypes with harmful repercussions.

Following attention to security, the marriage of home and land becomes temporarily disentangled in order to illustrate the mapping of land in relation to global space and the assertion of home in justifying attempts to conquer evil in chapter 3. Attention to land raises concern with the territorial constructions of the nation, seen as under threat by external forces of terrorism. These discussions are marked in terms of the position of the Middle East, particularly, as a source of fear, and yet largely unknown and misunderstood, particularly among avid fans and those who are not Arab American. The home is to be cherished and protected, and in relation to the nation becomes exemplified by the personification of the American ideal in the superhuman feats of these action-adventure heroes as explored in chapter 4. These heroes personify traits of the groups dominating U.S. culture, understood by informants as typically an European, American, Christian/secular, macho lone hero.

In the final chapter I consider a range of options for addressing the problematic media texts contributing to this spirit of oversimplified evil and conquest. As a first step, groups identify which films appear to be worth contesting; for example, recent action-adventure films designated as problematic by Arab American constituents include *True Lies*, *Executive Decision*, *The Siege*, *Die Hard*, *Rules of Engagement*, and *Air Force One* (EPIC/ MRI 2005; Hanania 1998), whereas CAIR and other groups have noted their support for Ridley Scott's *Kingdom of Heaven* (Goodale 2005). Strategies for addressing these problems include working within the industry, such as serving as consultants on film and television projects; working against the industry, such as advocating boycotts or protesting particular programs; or working in parallel to the mainstream media industry, such as establishing alternative media production and distribution systems.

Through the research presented in this book I hope to articulate how what we learn from action-adventure informs our perceptions of Arab communities. Documenting this link, however, falls short of the potential utility of research contributing toward public discourse and advocacy. We need to consider how to engage advocacy strategies at the sites of media production, through efforts to change industry practice as well as develop and distribute alternative media.

2

⁂

Fearing the "Other" in the Name of Security

The superior man, when resting in safety, does not forget that danger may come. When in a state of security he does not forget the possibility of ruin. When all is orderly, he does not forget that disorder may come. Thus his person is not endangered, and his States and all their clans are preserved.

—Confucius (551–479 BC)

As Americans, we want peace—we work and sacrifice for peace. But there can be no peace if our security depends on the will and whims of a ruthless and aggressive dictator. I'm not willing to stake one American life on trusting Saddam Hussein.

—George W. Bush (1946–), October 7, 2002

The ultimate security is your understanding of reality.

—H. Stanley Judd

Security signifies a sense of feeling safe and protected against potential attack or harm. As a social construction, security is informed through personal and social experience. But as a political construction, security becomes a symbolic code asserted in attempts to justify coercive interventions as integral to foreign policy as well as domestic strategies.

In establishing a U.S. Department of Homeland Security, President George W. Bush stated on November 8, 2001: "The government has a responsibility to protect our citizens, and that starts with homeland security" (USNHS 2007, 5). The mission of this department is to "lead the

25

unified national effort to secure America. We will prevent and deter terrorist attacks and protect against and respond to threats and hazards to the nation. We will ensure safe and secure borders, welcome lawful immigrants and visitors, and promote the free-flow of commerce" (USNHS 2007, 4). This campaign envelops security within a broader context of terrorist threat to the nation. The nation then becomes the privileged community worth protecting, along with the sanctified corporate sphere.

The fear accentuated in this political narrative resonates with the heightened sense of danger that builds suspense in action-adventure film. Danger becomes positioned as an external force that must be fought, avoiding recognition of internal threats within the national community. The boundaries of the nation are permeable, therefore justifying direct action within the territory as well as within global space. This external threat becomes manifest then in a fear of the "other," through the characterization of villains as distant from a normative center of power. A projection of difference reinforces the sense of a secure inner group, within the boundaries of a nation, against others, who are external to this constructed community.

These dichotomous characterizations of good and evil, embedded in political rhetoric within political speeches as well as within action-adventure film, essentialize a broad range of cultural shades into over simplified projections of light and dark in the characterization of heroes and villains. Like most dichotomies, this blending of shades of gray into rigid black-and-white parameters substitutes simplicity for recognition of complexity.

Although these mediated characterizations may be manifest within the texts of action-adventure film, how audiences engage this material may be quite different contingent on varied experiences and connections with the characters and settings portrayed. Given the established propensity of action-adventure film in relying on Arab characters as villains and Middle Eastern landscapes as mysterious and dangerous settings, this work explores how Arab American communities contrast with other U.S.-based communities in their construction of security issues, particularly in terms of their characterization and assessment of villains as well as their sense of fear and danger.

FEARING THE OTHER IN ACTION-ADVENTURE FILM

What we learn about villains through action-adventure films relates to our collective sense of fear within the context of establishing security. Villains represent external threats to security, personified as evil manifestations of this threat. How we interpret these villainous characters in the broader context of our political and social worlds needs to be explored.

Historically, Hollywood films have presented Arab characters more as villain than as victim or as hero, accentuating their distance from projected normative U.S. society by highlighting foreign accents, traditional clothing,[6] aggressive actions, and hostile attitudes (Elayan 2005; Shaheen 1984, 2001; Shohat and Stam 1994). Moreover, this cultural other, as exemplified in the comic *Captain America*, represents a vaguely drawn political georival to the United States (Dittmer 2005).

Next, discussions of villains are described in terms of how audiences characterize, remember, and assess them. The conflation and confusion across categories of ethnicity, nationality, and religion were quite striking in these focus group discussions. These distinctions will be teased out in this analysis, but it is worth recognizing that when subjects were asked specifically about one dimension, their responses often veered off into others, closely integrating Arab, Middle Eastern, and Muslim motifs. Characteristics divergent from the normative center seem to be universally recognized in relation to the portrayal of villains, though not uniformly appreciated.

Characterizing the Villain

In this section, audience constructions of action-adventure villains are explored, in descriptive as well as evaluative terms. Descriptions essentialize villainous characters as dehumanized "others," distant from the projected cultural center. Assessments of these portrayals range from assumptions that these are realistic and therefore justified to beliefs that these are stereotypical and therefore problematic. In contrast to discussions of the action-adventure hero as unidimensionally representing normative power in terms of ethnicity, nationality, religion, and gender, the villain counterposes these features, moving from the white and light to the dark and dirty.[7]

Not Human

One conceptual step in the process of accentuating fear relies on the dehumanization of villainous characters. Treating "others" (non-Europeans in Shohat and Stam's 1994 work) as less than human perpetuates a racist discourse in which villains are more easily destroyed. The dehumanization process accentuates the "animalistic" nature of villains, according to informants. Characters appear less human when not named and when appearing in groups, such that viewers are less likely to connect and identify with them.

First, viewers do not identify with villains in the same way as they are meant to with heroes. Not surprisingly, survey respondents are less likely to identify with villains (mean = 3.7 on 5-point scale with 5 marking strong disagreement) than with heroes (mean = 3.5) overall, though this difference is not nearly a broad as one might predict. More strikingly, the Arab American groups are much less likely to identify with the heroes (12 percent) than those in other groups (28 percent; gamma = 0.33), whereas neither group particularly identifies with the villains. Arab American groups register particular distaste for the Arab villain when describing these caricatures as insulting, monolithic, and inaccessible.

It's rare to find films in which viewers suggest they are able to identify with the villains. But when they do, it's notable. One Arab American participant marks *Three Kings* as one such film:

> *Three Kings* was a good example, how they gave a perspective to these people that were, the audience didn't really identify with, they gave them sort of an explanation for their motivation. It turned the whole movie around.

As part of this lack of identification, viewers appear less likely to recall names of characters or even of actors playing these characters than they do of heroes. People laughed in response to one person discussing Arnold Schwarzenegger in *True Lies* "against all these Arab terrorists. The funny thing is I can't remember the actor's name that played the main big bad guy. He's actually Indian." While most people could not remember names, others suggested that in action-adventure films, they "keep the villains nameless and they keep them from having a personality."

Connected with the lack of naming individual characters, many participants highlight the portrayal of villains in groups. The exception, noted across types of focus groups, is the White villain, elevated to individual status (such as Dennis Hopper in *Speed*); in contrast, Arab villains tend to approach scenes en masse. According to an Arab American participant, "When bad guys are Arab or Muslim, there's always a group of them. So it's easier to like stereotype when there's a group of people, versus in *Speed* it was one single person." Similarly, a participant in another group suggests that is "why it's so easy to kill all these people, because to us they don't have a face. They don't even have a serial number. Like you can't even pronounce their names."

Explanations for this appear to emphasize a projected sense of what audiences want:

> People usually don't want to humanize their enemy and see their side. So they like mindlessly watching these movies. They're like: see, we're right.

> In *True Lies*, there's, you know, you don't like these people because they're terrorists, and they're, you know, plotting to blow up America with nuclear weapons, so it's easy to watch them die and you don't feel bad that they die.

While informants across groups recognize the dehumanization of villainous characters, their evaluative judgments of the appropriateness of these characterizations differ greatly. The degree to which they perceive these portrayals as realistic or stereotypical will be addressed following further descriptions of villains through conceptual "othering."

The Non-White Foreigner

Viewers recognize the villain as typically removed from the White center of Middle America. The overriding sentiment is that villains tend to be "ethnic," meaning, "not White." This "othering" of ethnicity is closely connected with nationality, as "foreign" or "not American." One informant explains:

> What's the most easily defined scapegoat? I mean, darker people. It's always been darker people, especially in Texas. It doesn't matter if you're like shades or whatever, but like you want someone to make you uneasy right away, it's anybody who is a couple of shades darker than your average pillowcase.

Agreement also seems to persist that "the stereotypical villain in most part seems to be an Arab man." In descriptions of villains recalled, more than two-thirds (71 percent) of the research informants highlight Arab characters, also being the most frequently mentioned description (50 percent) of the "typical" villain's ethnicity. Arab American groups focus on their indignation with the Arab villains particularly. How does one "know" a character is "Arab"? One informant felt "insulted . . . you have no idea where these people are from, they look Indian, but they are supposed to be Arab, something like that. They kind of spout gobbledy gook that doesn't really mean anything, just syllables put together." Along with characters' speaking "Arabic [that] isn't very understandable," some informants point to the "beard" as indicative of Arab, terrorist status.

Appearance of facial hair seems connected in these discussions to descriptions of "dirty" and "ugly" male characters. Open-ended survey responses highlight villains' features as "dark," "non-White," "dirty," "ugly," "Eastern," or "Middle Eastern" men with facial hair and an "unpronounceable name," or as one put it, "creepy bearded Muslim extremists." As another informant explains:

> In general, most of the villains regardless of their ethnicity or anything else, they look different in some way, whether it's how they act, as opposed to others, how they look: they look dirty or something.

It is the notion of difference in projected ethnicity, through cues in appearance, which seems to matter in terms of viewer interpretation.

Markers of identity, through projected ethnicity as well as nationality, are conflated across focus group discussions as well as answers to open-ended survey questions. In terms of nationality, though, it is clear that the villain typifies the antithesis to the all-American hero. One of the most frequent responses to questions asking informants to describe the nationality of villains in action-adventure film is simply "not American" ($n = 29$), while some explicitly state that the villain is someone who "hates America."

About one-third of these descriptions refer specifically to Middle Eastern nationalities, while the remainder is split across a variety of regions. Arab American group participants are more likely than the others to recognize these national markers of Middle Eastern affiliations. When asked to recall specific villains, half of the Arab American group informants mark these characters as Middle Eastern compared with only 12 percent of the others; when asked to describe "typical" villains, this gap remained but narrowed, with just over a third (36 percent) of the Arab American and one quarter (24 percent) of the other informants explicitly using this categorization.

Both sets of focus groups frequently mention Russian and Middle Eastern origins of villains, and to a lesser extent South American and European backgrounds. The Arab American groups tend to be more specific in terms of their defined national identities, such as Palestinian, Yemeni, and Lebanese, as opposed to the more broadly defined "Middle Eastern" countries described by other groups, which are also more likely to suggest that the national identity be simply defined as "not American."

In discussions informants place current emphasis on Arab villains as contingent on historical context. Some define the 1980s as being the era of "Soviet" or "Russian" villains. Situating Russian or Japanese villains as more prominent in the past, one informant notes that "it sort of shifted to the Arab based. Or, I mean, Arab or darker-skinned people." This conceptualization excuses reliance on Arab terrorists as "just in this era, where it's either some raving lunatic madman or an Arab character." The following comments across informants demonstrate the extent to which historical context is meant to justify this positioning:

> Villains are mostly foreigners. Depends on what is going on with enemies of the U.S. Terrorists are Muslims and Arabs—a few years ago the Russians.

> They usually represent something, whatever the undeniably villainous force is in society at that moment. In the 1980s it was Russians. Now, well not now so much, but in the late 1990s it was Middle Easterners. Now, seems like there's this character I see a lot: the European mastermind.

I think the hostile history, that's what makes it believable. Because if someone made a movie about Belgium attacking us no one would . . . they'd be
like, is this a joke? The historical context is what makes it believable.

The justification of this context as being obvious, even "undeniable," suggests the normative power of this conceptualization.

Foreigners who "hate America" are believed to be "realistic" villains. In
one discussion of a "Palestinian" villain, his motives are dubbed "realistic" as "a guy harboring a deep hate in his life because his son or his children were killed in Palestine. . . . Since he's a Palestinian he's going to get
back at us."

"Outsiders," as one informant from a non–Arab American focus group
suggests, are to be feared. Because, as another put it, "Why would an
American want to bomb America? It just makes more sense to make it a
foreign person; I'm sure that's probably why they do it, even if it doesn't
make much sense." Foreigners make good terrorists, according to an Arab
American participant, particularly when they are "Arab or Muslim men
(with) . . . a large beard, . . . traditional outfits, . . . [and] hate the West."

Related to the cultural power of a normative center, Middle American
White culture also connotes a particular accent, against which other accents are deemed different and therefore distant. Accents appear to be a
distinguishing feature accentuating the "otherness" of Arabs, as well as
other types of characters, particularly those who are not American. The
following comments across different groups illustrate this concern:

They are just saying some Arabic terms, but it's like, gosh, what are they
doing?

It'd be like starting every Western scene with a Gregorian chant, I think.
Ghostly and old school. Just not what I think the reality is.

I think Arabic, to anyone that's not used to hearing it, it does sound harsh.
Like German does to me, whenever someone speaks in German, even my
aunts, they'll be really happy and talking and I always think they are mad.
To someone who has never listened to Arabic, if they raise their voice at all,
it sounds like they are very angry. It's very easy to have someone speak in
Arabic and play up that anger and make them seem hostile, I guess.

Distinguishing "accents" against normative Middle American English appears to be a recognizable feature among villains within the other non–Arab
American groups as well. Their comments concur with those of the others:

I'm watching *Alias* right now, I love that show, but all the bad guys have English accents and it's like they're making that "other."

Even if they are Americans they have a different accent—sometimes it's the way they talk.

The accent's the key to the villain part.

Muslim / Not Christian

Although religious affiliation of villains is not as frequently cited as ethnicity and nationality in responses to open-ended survey questions, when respondents do include such a notation, they consistently point to Muslim characters. The only exception is a response that describes villains as "any one who is NOT Christian." Islam and Christianity appear to be posed as dichotomous points, representing righteous heroes and evil villains, with little attention to other religious faiths or spiritual beliefs. Oversimplifying complex spiritual and secular beliefs, this dichotomization resonates with some of the arguments proposed to explain global conflict (Cloud 2004; Huntington 1996).

The integration of symbols of Islam with Arab characters from Middle Eastern countries is clear in many of the focus group discussions. Arab American groups frequently rehearse their concern with villains' appearance, clothing, chanting in Arabic, and praying to Allah. The way these scenes set a particular tone is noted in several discussions:

> They always use the call to prayers as setting the spooky tone in the movie—they have some crazy Muslim going: Allah!
> Then they'll have that rifle with them. They tie around their head like some scarf or something and they're ready to go all the time.
> Even like, this isn't action movies, but a PBS documentary, which is the nerdiness of me, trying to create a nice complex. It's still using like the call to prayer; it's used a lot to set the tone, then you get the sweep of the desolate geography, as if the Middle East is desert; it's very dry or the sun is just coming up; it gives you this ethereal feel to it.
> Chanting in Arabic.
> Yeah—chanting.

> I really dislike how those movies will show people praying and immediately afterward killing a bunch of people. To show these people really don't have any kind of faith and they kill indiscriminately.

> [They are] praying, right before they murder someone, they'll show them praying. You know, throwing out the prayer rug and then praying to Allah and then and going out.

> They are trying to show that Islam is violent.

The representation of religious faith in connection with Middle Eastern cultures is noted for its difference in comparison to villains from other non–North American regions.

> If you have a terrorist movie, where the villain is from South America or maybe a European country, the issue at the core isn't going to be religion, but money or drugs. But if you have a Middle Eastern villain, even if the issue is not religious, they always reemphasize it, yelling "Allah" over and over again or some random gibberish, or praying before a mass killing.

There are some striking differences across types of focus groups engaged in discussions of religious affiliations of villains. Arab Americans are generally more critical, pointing to differences between Arab Christians and Arab Muslims as a distinction "that is lost on most of the U.S." However, other participants are less likely to recall religious affiliations of villains at all, less likely to identify Islam explicitly, and more likely to attribute Christianity, particularly Catholicism among Irish characters. Some informants are not even sure how to refer to Islam, hinting at "some sort of Middle Eastern [religion], Allah."

The understanding of how Islam had been used to bolster the narrative within *The Siege* appeared to be lost for one informant:

> There's a scene in *The Siege* where the head of the terrorist cell and this chick who has been an Arabic scholar, and was actually sort of working with him because she's evil. And I remember that being the only discussion of the Koran I remember and it happens in this kind of Turkish bathhouse setting. I don't know where I'm going with this except this sort of, trying to express this topical, very superficial Islamic-ness, what was going on, was cosmetic Islam—I don't know.

In these discussions, some remarked that they felt pushed to identify any religious affiliation, not appearing to recall any attention to Islam. Excerpts from two of the other groups illustrate this point:

> I can think of, I can, honestly not a specific movie is coming to mind, but I can envision a scene in my head where it comes across really strongly.
> I can think of a few, not many.

> It's always American religions. You won't see an Arab villain worshipping an Islamic god. That would be attacking. I can't think of any Middle East villain with religion in an action movie.
>   I wonder if that's because they don't want to be offensive, because you're an American and that's your religion and they are affiliating your religion to the villain and that could be offensive to you, or they are just afraid to touch on religion.

Like I said, it's too deep.
I agree.

Another participant explained the potential discomfort he believes people feel in relation to Christian proselytizers in relation to potentially vocal Muslims:

There were some people on the bus coming up here that started shouting about Jesus really loud. I got off the bus and as soon as they got off they started yelling at everybody. . . . I didn't say anything to them, I figure they can say what they want but I think it has to do with what you were saying, that we tend to see that, we let some people get away with it and that's okay. We'll let them do their thing down at the mall. We're not going to say anything even if they are shouting and beating on the Bible. But if someone was shouting from the Koran, I don't know, it might create a problem.

Moreover, confusion seems to reign in some of these other focus group discussions concerning the particular goals of Islam in relation to terrorism, while recognizing the dangers of basing assumptions on stereotypes:

They make terrorism usually so religion specific, but only when it applies to, like, the Arabs, or the Muslims. We've made, like, progress in saying, like, different treating, you know, like maybe in the '80s or a little bit before it was Arabs, and now at least it's, like, Saudis, Egyptians, you know, Israelis, Iraqis, whatever. And that's good: we have figured out the use of name tags, like which one is which, but, like, movies like this, because they use religion-specific terrorists, they supply the terror. That's the only thing that drives me nuts is that they make terror by making all of them clones of one another. I mean, so when stuff like this happens, you think . . . or like the Oklahoma City bombing [another group participant vocalizes agreement here], where was the first finger pointed? Muslim fundamentalists, you know? I don't think there's been a terrorist attack in the media in the last two years where they haven't said it was, like, an Islamic jihadist claimed responsibility, you know? Like, I don't know necessarily if these people are just claiming responsibility just to claim responsibility, either. . . . I mean, I see it as a flaw in the media too, but they're not getting a good word out, you know?

These voiced experiences confronting Christian as well as Muslim advocates, whether through the media or in person, illustrate the degree to which informants recognize Islam as threatening, and Christianity as more comprehensible and far from ominous. These discussions illustrate the power of the normative center, along with the marginality and fear of the periphery, whether addressing religious affiliation, nationality, ethnicity, or gender.

Dirty Men / Beautiful Women

Across groups, participants ascribe the typical villain as male, yet recognizing that in films recalled most (86 percent) but not all are male as well. The themes generated across these discussions point to dirty, ugly men, juxtaposed with beautiful women using their sexuality as a tool, consistent with portrayals of women as heroes as well.

Male villains are often described in connection with being Arab, Muslim, and bearded. Female villains, on the other hand, are "very sexy if they are from a third world country." Even the "White chick" in *The Siege* "who's gone to the dark side [was] . . . kind of an unrealistic character because I can see no reason why a Harvard-educated White chick would want to convert to fundamentalist Islam."

One participant explains the gender differences in villains:

> I guess if you look statistically, most crimes are committed by men, but women can commit crimes too. But you have a different type of female, like with the male villains you have a couple types. You have crazy guy, which is usually White male serial killer guy, [who] wants to kill a bunch of people, kind of Ted Kaczynski mind-set, usually fears technology, that sort of thing. You know, that guy. And then you have the terrorists, you know, someone with a political aim. Actually they seem to be pretty good at showing different kinds of terrorists: they're not all Middle Eastern, they have, like, IRA-type people, I know on *Air Force One,* I think they were Chechnian [*sic*] or something like that?

> But with the women, you have like the evil seductress type of villain is usually what you have. She's always using her sexuality as a weapon, you don't have a nerdy plotting female, unless you're watching *Monster,* but even she used her sexuality and that wasn't an action movie. But, I can't think, well, in *Kill Bill,* there were female villains and they were assassins, but again they're wearing catsuits and whatnot and shimmying about and you don't have that so much with the men.

With some distinction across groups' characterizations of villains' religious affiliations, otherwise the sense of villains as nonhuman, foreign "others" dominates these discussions. These characterizations project senses of fear, based in part on particular memories of villains portrayed in action-adventure film.

Remembering the Villain

Focus group dialogue about villains in the six most frequently discussed films illustrates how these tropes become manifest in specific discussions. Each group selected a few films to discuss as a group based on individual

responses to survey questions. These six represent the five most frequently discussed films among Arab American and other focus groups.
These groups corresponded on the first four most frequently described,
including, in order of popularity, *True Lies*, *Air Force One*, *Die Hard*, and
The Sum of All Fears, but differed in the fifth film, being *The Siege* for Arab
Americans and *Speed* for the other participants. Memory of these particular villains in relation to the text confirms the patterns evidenced in
broader discussions of the genre.

The central villain in *Air Force One*, played by Gary Oldman, portrays a
Caucasian male soldier from Kazakhstan heading a group acting out of
revenge for their leader's capture and prison sentence. Apart from one
European American secret service collaborator, the other secondary villains were similar to the central villain, Ivan Korshunov. Unlike descriptions of the film's hero, informants were less likely to focus on the actor's
name and not at all on the character's name. Instead, descriptions focused
on villains in their role as terrorists, but even more so in terms of their nationality or ethnicity. Importantly, memories of these villains are not entirely accurate: while the terrorists were situated as emerging from a resistant group in Kazakhstan fighting against the Russian government,
most people described these villains as Russian, Eastern European, Arab,
or foreign.

The film *Speed* illustrates another White, though American, male villain,
Howard Payne, played by Dennis Hopper. This character acts alone, inspired to embark on revenge against the police department that had employed him. Most informants describing this character focused on him as
"crazy." Very little attention was given to his name or his ethnicity. Similarly, descriptions of Alan Rickman's villainous character Hans Gruber in
Die Hard avoided discussions of the actor's name or his ethnicity, instead
concentrating more on his national identity. Most of these depictions correctly pointed to these villains as German or European, but a few labeled
them as Russian. National distinctions also dominated discussions of
"neo-Nazi" villains in *The Sum of All Fears*, coming from Austria, Russia,
South Africa, and the United States. Informants recalled these villains
mostly as German, Russian, or Eastern European. Although this film did
include Arab arms traders facilitating the work of the terrorists, discussions did not acknowledge these secondary characters. It is worth noting
the change in villains' backgrounds from the originally ordained Islamic
extremists in Tom Clancy's novel to the neo-Nazi figures featured in the
film, which was produced prior to 9/11.

Two of the other films discussed at length by these groups, *The Siege*
and *True Lies*, featured Arab villains. While the majority of respondents focused their descriptions of the villains on the Arab Muslim characters, *The
Siege* also includes military personnel in duplicitous roles, recognized by

some but not many informants as villainous. One of the respondents reported that she included *The Siege* in her discussion "because that's my favorite action-adventure film about terrorism and it scared the crap out of me when I saw it, less than because of the Islamic terrorists and more because of the military state."

Most discussions and descriptions of *The Siege* focused on the Muslim, Arab, or Middle Eastern characteristics of villains. A central villain, Nazhde, offers a potential vehicle for these discussions portraying an Arab Muslim with U.S. and Palestinian national affiliations. Similarly, discussions of *True Lies* emphasized the Arab, Muslim, and Middle Eastern features of the terrorist groups, but in vague terms (as just "foreign" at times), rather than concretely describing Art Malik as Salim Abu Aziz, or even referring to Tia Carrere's character Juno Skinner, an art dealer/arms trader of mixed descent. Critics and scholars alike highlight this film for "Reinforc[ing] the image of the Arab as an inimical other" (Eisele 2002, 88).

However, informants made several mistakes in terms of their memories of these villains. With reference to *True Lies,* one informant refers to the terrorist as Indian/Arab. In discussions of *The Siege,* one mistakenly refers to the Nazhde character as Iraqi, and another describes the Tony Shalhoub character, portraying a heroic figure supporting Denzel Washington, specifically as a villain. Some confusion in recalling good guys as distinct from bad guys may emanate from what one informant explained as the complexity of the story: "*The Siege* was the greatest movie ever made by Hollywood, maybe, in terms of dealing with the Middle East. Even though the heroes were American soldiers, one of them African American, they were conflicted about what they were doing, they were trying to do the right thing and wrong thing at the same time, and there were no clear-cut bad guys in the movie."

Even when portrayals of character backgrounds within film texts exhibit variation and complexity, audience memory privileges Arab and Muslim features over others when recalling specific villains, particularly within the Arab American focus groups. Moreover, the confusion across Arab and Muslim communities, specifically emphasizing radical features of Islam, exemplifies discussions of characterized terrorists. While the nationality of the hero tends to be assumed to be American, the nationalities of villains are more clearly articulated as foreign.

Cultural memory of particular groups as being cast in heroic and villainous roles is predicated on the broader Orientalist discourse in which these texts and discussions are situated. Multiple respondents pointed out that the groups cast as villains seem to change depending on the time in which the films are made, for example, seeing a number of Russian or Japanese villains in the past, but noting that "it sort of shifted to the Arab based. Or, I mean, Arab or darker-skinned people." Even though fewer villains are explicitly Arab or Muslim in recent Hollywood films (Salam 2002), articulation of these communities in this role still dominates memory. Memories of the specific characteristics of villains appear to inform beliefs of typical villains. Assessments of villains are grounded on these characterizations. The hegemonic discourse that excuses the projection of the Arab, Muslim villain does not permeate all discussions in the same way. Particularly among Arab Americans, there is strong resistance and concern.

Assessing the Villain

In addition to describing key features of specific villains recalled as well as of those projected to be typical, informants offered some assessment of these characters. While some considered these villains as realistic, others critiqued them as being overly simplistic.

Realistic

While groups may have agreed on some of the essential features describing villains, their judgments of these portrayals differ in significant ways, such as the extent to which characterizations were deemed realistic. Participants in non–Arab American groups are more likely than their counterparts to justify the representation of Arab villains as realistic. These discussions are provocative, however, with participants challenging one another's assumptions, as in the following case:

> I would be a liar if I were to tell you that all nineteen of the hijackers on September 11th weren't Arab. That's a reality. But in the same sense, that doesn't mean that Arabs took part in the bombing of the Oklahoma City federal building.
>
> So we can say yes, it's realistic, because it has happened.
>
> But no, it's not realistic that it's always going to happen.
>
> It's not always going to be them, yeah.
>
> Right.
>
> And the vast majority of movies portray them as the people coming and taking over and being bad, bad men. And neither are all Arab women like belly dancers.
>
> They're not?
>
> No!
>
> [Laughter.]
>
> I was surprised myself.

Other groups reflect this tension as to whether Arab villains were realistic. In one group, the statement that villains being "Arab and Muslim, just because after 9/11 and even prior to the WTC bombing and the history of airplane hijackings and so forth. . . . It's wrong to say there have not been Arabs committing terrorist acts" is followed by disagreement. In response, an informant explains that the "terrorist acts we hear about in the media are usually committed by Arabs, but stereotypical kinds of representations come in [and] you're not given any kind of context as to why they are committing these acts."

Another participant in a non–Arab American group elaborates this point:

> As much as I hate to say it, using the terrorists, like, the Middle Eastern, like, ah, like suicide bomber things like that, I would almost say that is, that, you know, maybe not deep down but at least on the surface that is realistic to me, just because of what's going on now and what the media exposes and with the suicide bombings, and with Osama bin Laden and everything going on there. So, if I want to think terrorists, naturally I would admit that that's what comes to mind. So pardon me for that, but that is realistic to me.

These assessments of villains as realistic, particularly when manifest in Arab, Muslim, or Middle Eastern features, figure more prominently in the other focus groups but not among the Arab American groups, in which the discussion focused much more directly on critique.

Simplistic

In contrast, Arab American participants are much more cognizant of the portrayal of Arab villains as a critical concern. Frequently their critiques of the "one-dimensional" nature of Arab villains led to suggestions that action-adventure films do more to develop the depth of these characters.

> I don't think I ever saw a terrorist film that tried to show anything about the villain's side, or the villain's story. Not even a bias about being Arab, just in general if you make a movie—it's a bad movie if they aren't developing all the characters. They have a somewhat developed hero, maybe, in that he's the common man, but you have absolutely nothing to identify with the villain, strictly good guys and strictly bad guys and nobody else. I feel they don't develop the villains at all and that makes it very unrealistic.

While the concern with the portrayal of Arabs as villains seems universally shared among the Arab American focus groups, discussions of this subject in other groups are much more far ranging, from vague concern with stereotyping in general to more blatant acceptance. The following excerpt from a focus group discussion illustrates how participants attempt to make sense of how media stereotyping might affect their lives:

> You don't go, you wake up every morning, pick up your mail and say, "Oh, I hate Arabs, give me some coffee." It's just kind of one of those things like it just, it's put into your mind and after a while you get uneasy if somebody, like, implies that they're Arab or Muslim or anything else. It's just kind of, that is real. Like they're more moved by it than by everyday life, that is real.
>
> I think it's very akin to if I, if you see an Arab walking down the street, what's your first reaction? I personally, personally I smile, because I'm glad they're out there. And if I see an African American on the street. . .
>
> How do you know he's Arab, though? [interrupting previous speaker]
>
> I mean, how do I know he's [indicates other participant] from Mexico?
>
> You don't!
>
> You see it . . . it's not . . . like but the point being is, some people . . . do you reach for your wallet and kind of run or do you take a step back? It's very similar to how you see a movie. If I see a villain that's Arabic, I don't necessarily associate that villain with every Arab.

In these other non–Arab American groups, the concern is not with the representation of Arab culture specifically, but directed toward stereotyping more generally. One informant recognizes that "Arabs get a terrible, terrible deal in the way they're portrayed, ... forty years ago, if you were Black you were eating a watermelon and smiling," with another immediately responding: "While playing dominoes and tap dancing." A complex interplay permeates these discussions, in which informants both appear to assume that equating terrorism with Middle Eastern/Arab/Muslim cultures is acceptable, yet recognizing issues of racism and stereotypes more broadly. The following statement made in a focus group discussion exemplifies these tensions:

> We also tend to associate terrorism with the Middle East these days and you have a very narrow-minded definition of terrorism and if you kind of broaden that definition to include all acts of terror, committed by all kinds of people, such as racism that existed in the U.S. for years, then you have a whole category of terrorist movies that kind of opens up when you think about it.

Many members of these non—Arab American groups recognize the issue of stereotyping as a problem in representation of villains more broadly. Terrorists, particularly, rely on simplistic characterizations without context:

> They tend to make them seem more single-minded, you know, it makes them seem very stupid usually, which granted I mean I'm not going to say that terrorists are well-educated, enlightened folks that know what's up, but they often, it seems like they don't know very many words and stuff like that. But again, I don't, I mean it makes it seem very simplified and I imagine that if you, I mean no one's going to explore the motivations of why this person feels the need to bomb America or whatever.

While understanding the problems of stereotyping, particularly among villainous characters, more broadly, some of these focus group members explicitly deny that the issue need be of particular concern to Arab or Middle Eastern communities. However, when one participant remarked that "it's easy to *say* these films stereotype Middle Easterners but I haven't seen one yet," others disagreed.

Arab American focus groups, much more than the others, focused on the need for more complexity and context in order to understand the motivations of villains. Characters being too "simple" or "cartoonish" were considered particularly problematic. Several referenced Palestinian historical conditions as an area particularly absent in portrayals of Arab terrorists.

FEARING THE OTHER IN THE NAME OF SECURITY

Characterizing villains accentuates the "otherness" of these characters, deemed realistic by some and problematic by others. Positioned as the antithesis of the light, White, all-American Christian man, the evil, dehumanized darker foreign masses threaten peace, stability, and individual freedom. The ability to recall the particular characteristics of villains seems contingent on the extent to which viewers are concerned with the stereotypical and simplistic aspects of these portrayals; otherwise, memory of villains can be suspiciously in tune with dominant prejudicial attitudes within the society rather than specifically referencing ethnic, national, or religious attributes evidenced in films.

Even when portrayals of character backgrounds within film texts exhibit variation and complexity, audience memory privileges Arab and Muslim features over others when recalling specific villains. Moreover, the confusion across Arab and Muslim communities, specifically emphasizing radical features of Islam, exemplifies discussions of characterized terrorists. The villains, particularly when ascribed Arab and

Muslim dimensions, accentuate the exoticism and difference of these communities, typically operating in dehumanized groups, wearing traditional clothes, and chanting and praying in Arabic. These types of critiques were much less apparent among the other focus groups. Even the recognition of the typically Muslim character of Middle Eastern villains featured in Arab American focus groups is found much less often in discussions of other groups', which instead are more likely to believe that villains at times instituted Christian themes. Again, although the questions guiding focus group discussions attempt to disentangle ethnic from national and religious affiliations, it is important to note the conflation of these categories in the course of normative discussion within the groups.

These groups also differ in the extent to which the plots and explanations for villainous acts are seen as over simplified. The Arab American groups are more likely to advocate for more complexity within the narrative structure, in order to offer historical context as well as some explanation for the frustration and anger that may have inspired the villains. Some of the terms raised in these discussions include giving the "other side of the story," or the "alternative" perspective, and "avoiding clichés." Their concerns with the dominant perspective recognize the connections between villainous caricatures in media and everyday experiences with prejudice.

Security becomes a central justification for transforming fear of the other into particular polices and practices that harm those who are believed to be associated with groups responsible for terrorist acts. Prejudicial claims against individuals and groups are less concerned with respecting particular people or communities, and instead more reactive to the dominant stereotypes evoked in action-adventure narratives. Mapping fear of others, as villains, also needs to be understood within the context of particular places and spaces, and is addressed in the next chapter.

3

Mapping Land and Fear in Global Space

A man's homeland is wherever he prospers.

> —Aristophanes (450–388 BC), *Plutus*, 388 BC

This England never did, nor never shall,
Lie at the proud foot of a conqueror.

> —William Shakespeare (1564–1616), *King John*, act 5 scene 7

America is therefore the land of the future, where, in the ages that lie before us, the burden of the World's History shall reveal itself.

> —Georg W. Hegel (1770–1831)

Building on the previous chapter addressing concerns with security, next I consider the constructions of the aspect of "land," within the broader interest in "homeland." In essence security encompasses a need to protect, whether this be a tangible set of possessions, feeling of inner tranquility, or territorial space. It is this final category that becomes privileged in discussions of homeland security, equating a territorial sense of the nation-state with a particular patriotic sense of identity in relation to this territory as "home." The land itself grounds the work of national security, as policies and programs are enacted to establish boundaries that allow entry to particular legal immigrants as well as certain sanctioned goods, but prevent the passage of other people and products that are deemed either illegal or potentially facilitating terrorist attack. Land as territory becomes what is to be protected in a tangible sense, but also confers a sense of allegiance to this construction of the nation.

Visions of land associated with the nation become pronounced in mediated narratives, as well as institutionalized through the establishment of the U.S. Department of Homeland Security. The "homeland" requiring security within the United States fosters patriotic images of national flags, uniforms, and urban landscapes, as evidenced in the published literature establishing this department within the United States (USDHS 2007). These landscapes, along with other images, evoke vivid portrayals meant to inspire pride in national symbols, with the underlying sense that this homeland should be cherished and protected at all costs.

The construction of a homeland positions a particular territory within a broader global context. The territorial boundaries of the homeland project a sense of a national community grounded within a defined area. While diasporic communities may reside outside of this territory, there remains a sense of connection and identification with a particular area. How we create maps of our "land" engages a sense of cultural community tied to a particular territorial space, within a broader global context.

This chapter explores how Arab American and other U.S.-based communities map place within global space, in relation to fear, through their engagement with action-adventure film. The connotations associated with particular places, delineating national homeland from foreign territories, particularly the Middle East in these dialogues, ground projected fears of terrorism and travel within conceived comfortably close as well as dangerously distant lands.

Mapping land within global space articulates a vision of cultural communities and boundaries that allows us to situate our own position within a broader sociopolitical context. While the map may indeed not be the territory, as so cogently argued by Gregory Bateson (1972), mapping is how we come to make sense of our world. Cultural mapping creates a context in which our mobility and our interpretations are guided along particular paths. Maps connote images that demarcate and categorize disparate information, in ways that essentialize differences and guide directions that suggest some routes while avoiding others. Mapping involves more than individually created subjective experiences, but builds on intersubjectively understood decisions, engaged as conventional wisdom.

The processes of media production and reception embody cultural mapping, in that mediated constructions create codes that function as stereotypical plots, settings, and characters. The mediated mapping of cultural groups and distant territories takes on even more relevance when relating those communities and places outside of our daily experiences. The act of constructing a territory we refer to as the "Middle East" produces a category envisioned from a particular historical and political perspective. Critics of mediated constructions of this territory point to the lack of historical and political context accorded this region, as well as the simplified, stereotypical versions of this landscape.

The analysis presented here attempts to demonstrate how "geopolitical truth" becomes established given "physical claims to space" (Dittmer 2005, 641). Domination in global space is contingent on this projected legitimacy of state institutions in addressing agents of terror. Dittmer's (2005) study of the now defunct comic *Captain America* demonstrates how this text projects the primacy of the nation-state within the global geopolitical system as a way of organizing global space. Even more importantly, his analysis confirms the projection of American nationalism, rooted in White, Christian Middle America, working to thwart potential threats from foreign terrorists associated with Islam. Moreover, the Middle East itself offers a "unifying narrative" that builds on a "long-standing European tradition of using the East as a sounding board for the creation of myths of identity" (Eisele 2002, 91). Attention to the Middle East as a particular setting needs to be understood first within the broader context of global space articulated in discussions of action-adventure film settings.

MAPPING PLACE

In the first section of this chapter, I explore how research participants describe their memories of specific film settings they have seen, as well as those they project in "typical" action-adventure films. Analyses considered here build from focus group discussions of the narratives and settings of particular films as well as idealized versions of the action-adventure genre. In discussions and in surveys, informants were asked to describe remembered and ideal settings, as well as their experiences and attitudes concerning foreign travel, personal and national security, global events, and terrorism. Their answers to open-ended questions at times indicate specific geographical places, and other times indicate broadly composed spaces, suggesting themes such as dark urban or sandy desert landscapes.

Overall, their references to settings in specific films and in typical films demonstrate similar conceptualizations of constructed territories. Most places recalled and projected in action-adventure film are within the United States (79–84 percent). Among the foreign areas listed however, the "Middle East" is highlighted more frequently than any other area. One key difference when describing other foreign settings is that for typical films these answers refer more generically to "foreign" settings (13 percent) and if not that then definitively the "Middle East" (8 percent), whereas films recalled tend to designate specific territories in the Middle East (6 percent),

Asia (6 percent), and Africa (4 percent). Answers referring to "foreign" settings are also frequently accompanied by terms such as "exotic" and "dark." The "exotic" theme is also carried through in the broader descriptions of settings, which rely on Orientalist themes focusing on either "sandy," "dusty" "deserts" with "camels," particularly "when dealing with a terrorist," or on dark crowded East Asian urban settings.[8]

While groups recognize settings similarly in terms of "typical" films, their recall of settings in films they had seen differed, with Arab American groups being more likely to mention Middle Eastern settings (8 percent) than the other groups (3 percent). Given this disparity in attention and memory, it follows that the nature of their critiques and justifications differ considerably.

Arab American groups are quite critical of Middle Eastern scenes, wanting more realistic, complex situations. In their discussions, they register concern with an overreliance on settings in deserts with camels, groups of people in "traditional" outfits, unexplained violence, and unrealistic backgrounds. The Middle Eastern settings appear to them as unnecessarily backward and foreign, dark and mysterious. Instead of specific Arab places, a more generic backdrop with key features is meant to indicate this region: "They don't say what country you are in, but they have the checkered head cloth." Arab cities are portrayed as lacking electricity, as well as indications of Western and global culture, such as commercial advertising. The spoken language is often noted to sound like nonsense, and written script is used to accentuate the distance between the film scene and dominant American culture.

Instead, Arab American groups suggest that more realistic settings would include a variety of urban as well as rural conditions, with characters speaking in Arabic correctly, wearing a variety of clothing. In addition, they advocate for symbols of Western and global integration, such as Coke signs, as evidence of U.S. political and economic involvement in the region.

A central concern raised in these discussions is that while the informants themselves might understand how unrealistic these representations of the Middle East might be, others would not:

> When a group of my friends go see a movie like that, that's the image they have, especially when they show a scene in the Middle East, or in South America. It's just frustrating because I can watch that and know it's not all like that. I'm lucky enough to be like that. But the people I know don't have that luxury, and they'll be like: oh, not everyone is like that, or not every country is run that way, not all Muslims are terrorists. But, they don't, it's hard, you can't, they don't expose people to other sides, not to where there is a balance of it. It's one sided.

While other focus groups described a variety of foreign settings, when they circled around Middle Eastern venues they saw an advantage in accentuating the exotic aspect of these backgrounds. For example, they describe the setting in Yemen in the film *Rules of Engagement* as realistic as well as exotic, and thus appropriate for an action-adventure film.

Next, analyses focus specifically on how the settings of the six most frequently discussed action-adventure films were recalled by participants, in relation to discussions in focus groups of particular films. These are discussed in alphabetical order.

The first film, *Air Force One* (1997), portrays the heroic feats of U.S. president James Marshall when terrorists hijack his plane and kill passengers. The film takes place primarily in the interior of the Air Force One plane, but also includes scenes in Washington, D.C., Russia, and Kazakhstan. Almost all (94 percent) of the informants describing the setting of this film focus on the plane itself, while only one mentions the geographical setting of Washington, D.C. The other foreign territories are absent from these discussions.

The next film, *Die Hard* (1988), centers its action on a New York policeman who saves hostages, including his wife, from terrorists. This film was the third most popular film raised in discussions. While almost half (42 percent) correctly identified the setting as Los Angeles or an office building, many thought the film was set in New York (42 percent) or some other city (17 percent).

The film *The Siege* (1998) is included in discussions of action-adventure films more by the Arab Americans than the other participants, often as a way of illustrating their concerns with the genre. In this film, terrorists attack New York City, met by the competitive forces from the CIA and FBI. The film features internment camps as well as other scenes in New York City, with some scenes situated in the Saudi desert. All informants correctly identify this staging in New York City, with one also remembering the scene in the Middle East. Her description emphasizes the nature of the scene as

so cartoonish that, I mean, there's one thing, it really looked like *Aladdin*— they are going through the desert in this Mercedes and you see the leader and he's sitting in the backseat but he's not even sitting in the passenger side—he's sitting between the two, so you have him all in white, sitting between these two black seats, so he's even put in the position between two black seats which looks awkward yet evil. It really looks like *1001 Nights*, *Arabian Nights* setting, it's just really, I can't even believe it's a real movie.

In *Speed* (1994), a retired police officer plants a bomb on a bus that will explode when its speed falls below fifty miles an hour. The setting of this film is mostly in the bus in Los Angeles; the informants correctly remember both the city and the vehicle.

The Sum of All Fears (2002) portrays a young CIA agent working against terrorists attempting to agitate a war between the United States and Russia. This film situates action in a variety of settings, including Washington, D.C., and Baltimore, along with Austria, Russia, Ukraine, Israel, and Syria. The most commonly recalled setting among informants is Washington, D.C. (58 percent). Others describe the setting more generically as the United States (33 percent) or Europe (8 percent). Some note foreign locations in Russia (33 percent) or Israel (8 percent).

The film *True Lies* (1994) chronicles the story of a U.S. special government agent working to keep terrorists from launching nuclear bombs on the United States. This film is set in a variety of places, including Switzerland, Washington, D.C., the Florida Keys, and Miami. Most informants describe the United States (52 percent), Washington, D.C. (17 percent), or Florida (9 percent) as the film's location. Others specify non-U.S. locations, including France, the Caribbean, Europe, or simply refer to "foreign" or "international" locations.

Discussions of these specific films confirm patterns established in relation to the genre more broadly. The confusion over the nature of foreign villains described in the previous chapter resonates with recall of film settings: memory of U.S.-based venues is more prevalent than that of foreign places, while many have difficulty naming particular places outside of the United States, instead relying on more generalized and vague regional descriptions. The specific historical context or political instance matters less than a broader, comprehensive sense of fear of that which is different, rooted in foreign territory.

Mapping the Middle East

Thus far, this mapping of global space brings the U.S. landscape into sharp focus while obscuring foreign settings into vague, hazy backdrops. Arab American groups, though, appear much more cognizant of and concerned with the particular portrayal of the Middle East within this context than the other participants. In many ways, the characterization of the Middle East as a particular setting builds on a lack of knowledge and a preponderance of fear.

Knowledge of the Middle East

Indeed, knowledge of the Middle East appears to be limited among intensive action-adventure fans. Within the survey, informants were asked questions to ascertain relative knowledge of recent events in the region. A scale assessing knowledge was composed of answers agreeing or dis-agreeing with the following statements: Israeli Prime Minister Rabin was assassinated by a Palestinian (mean = 3.6 on a 5-point Likert scale, with 5 representing strongly disagree); the UN has repeatedly condemned Israel for occupying other people's land (mean = 2.3); the federal building in Oklahoma was bombed by Arab Americans (mean = 4.7); and Saddam Hussein did have weapons of mass destruction in Iraq (mean = 4.1; alpha = 0.55; eigenvalue = 1.7 predicting 43 percent of the variance).

Those who are more consistently action-adventure fans do appear to know less about the region (50 percent gaining a high knowledge score) than those who are not (65 percent). This relationship holds moderate strength (gamma = -0.31). However, the effects of group identity may be suppressing stronger effects. While this pattern is maintained among other participants (46 percent of this group with low exposure had high levels of knowledge compared with 39 percent of those with high film ex-posure), this trend falls away among Arab American group constituents (78 percent compared with 81 percent have high levels of knowledge). It's worth noting too that overall participants in the Arab American groups are much more knowledgeable (80 percent scoring in the highest cate-gory) than their counterparts in other groups (42 percent; gamma = -0.61). By implication, those with the least knowledge are participants in other groups who are intensive fans of the genre.

It is not clear whether intensive fans of this genre happen to be more knowledgeable, or whether those who watch these films learn about the region differently. While the particular causal direction of this connection cannot be assessed through cross-sectional research, the clear correlation between exposure to this genre and knowledge of the region is worth noting.

Fear of the Middle East

Building on this lack of knowledge, projected fear of the Middle East is also predicated on direct experience in as well as family connections with the region. Moreover, intensive consumption of action-adventure con-tributes to this fear. The consistently problematic portrayals of Arab vil-lains, while well documented, have critical repercussions in the attitudes of U.S.-based viewers.

Fear of the Middle East and of Arab communities was assessed in rela-tion to action-adventure viewing through participants' survey responses. Extent of fear was considered through levels of agreement to the following statements: The main enemies in the United States are based in the Middle East (mean = 3.5 on a 5-point scale); most of the terrorist acts in the United States are committed by Arabs (mean = 4); and U.S. military intervention in the Iraq is justified (mean = 4.5; alpha = 0.65; eigenvalue = 1.8 predicting 59 percent of the variance).

Within this community of viewers, those who are more likely to consume action-adventure films are much more likely to hold high levels of this fear than those who see fewer films of this genre. More than twice as many (27 percent) intensive action-adventure fans rank highly on this scale compared with those with low exposure (10 percent); in contrast, more than half of those (52 percent) with low exposure have low rates of this specific fear compared with 40 percent of those with high exposure. This relationship appears to have moderate strength (gamma = 0.29).

The next set of questions pertains to other factors that might mediate between media exposure and attitudes, such as cultural identification and experience. Given the substantive issues of these analyses, controlling for type of focus group, which correlates directly with personal identification with Arab culture as well as direct experience in the Middle East, further accentuates these findings. Overall, the relationship between exposure to action-adventure films and fear of Arab communities and the Middle East becomes more pronounced among non-Arab groups: the proportion of those with the highest levels of fear are among those with high consumption of this genre among other groups, with a striking difference of 29 percent compared with 8 percent among those in these groups who do not consume this genre. The trend among the Arab focus groups is similar, in that 22 percent with high exposure hold this fear compared with 13 percent with low exposure, but the difference is less stark.

Contrary to expectations, when we examine the bivariate connection between type of group and level of fear, we see that the differences are not that great, with 16 percent of Arab American groups and 21 percent of other groups exhibiting these tendencies (gamma = 0.0). This makes the interaction between genre consumption and type of group all the more striking.

Yet participants in these groups feel the consequences of this prejudicial fear quite differently. One of the Arab American focus group participants articulates his concern that the effects of villainizing Arab communities are far reaching into U.S. society, affecting citizens as well as policy:

> I think these films successfully instill fear in Americans, and reinforce the idea that the villains are Arab Americans that have very real repercussions in society that we don't . . . these films are part of a larger discourse which is basically kind of, they add to the justification for the things that are going on now. Just like with what's going on with Iraq and that Bush did what he did and there are not WMDs found and I think film is kind of part of that discourse, these types of films. I think that they are very problematic, they are not just for entertainment, they have serious repercussions.

Viewers do appear to justify problematic characterizations of villains in ways that resonate with the broader cultural conditions in which these films are produced and distributed. First, there is the assumption that the "average American wants to see good versus evil." Elaborating further, another informant explains: "The average, you know, people go to movies for escape: they want to see definite good and evil; they want to see somebody win and somebody lose; they want to know who to root for."

Moreover, an us/Unived States-versus-them/other mentality permeates justifications, particularly among non–Arab American participants. One such informant believes:

> Our movies are so offensive to them because we always show them as the enemy and how, you know, they live by a lot stricter moral code, how our women walk around uncovered and the things they wear and things like that.

In sum, among those in the other focus groups, the division of what "we" want and like in contrast to what is assumed "others" practice and preach places the recognized problematic stereotypical representations of villains and settings within a realm of conventionally understood brackets. The norms justifying what would seem problematic across other ethnic, racial, religious groups are used to excuse the consistently narrow portrayal of the Arab, Muslim villains in Middle Eastern settings.

MAPPING FEAR AND TERROR

Fear relies not only on a projected character, but also on more obscure senses of danger lurking in particular types of places and spaces. For some, fear becomes articulated in an external territory, such as the Middle East, while for others, it arises in particular types of spaces, such as airports.

When informants are asked what countries they would like to avoid when traveling, the range of answers in non–Arab American groups is wide, but centers on the Middle East, with comments like "of course," and "especially." Discussions concur, without much disagreement, that the "Middle East" should be avoided, because in one participant's words: "I wouldn't want to put myself in a situation where I would be running for my life." One specifically notes a concern with "Islamic terrorists, like Hamas, Hezbollah, the various authorities that on a fairly frequent basis target Americans." In one of these groups, a divergent voice explains a lack of fear of the Middle East because she had "several Persian friends, so I'm not afraid of Middle Eastern people. One of them is Christian, but they are all normal."

Connections to mediated experiences surface in these conversations. One describes an "action-adventure feeling that Americans get when they are in other countries. I feel as if that sort of danger, Americans in particular feel like they can overcome it, they are immune to it, they can do whatever they want in these countries and that spirit gets us in a lot of trouble." Another informant in the same conversation notes that

> action movies are central to American culture. Americans have always loved spaghetti Westerns, that sort of thing. We Americans in particular favor this particular genre over other countries because this country has been one huge action-adventure film from the Revolutionary War to exploring out West. Our cultural definition is going farther in the future, we don't look at the past. Like in most of the countries in the world you reflect on your nationality. Here we have nationality but we are a very progress-oriented society. We like adventure and we like action.

Someone in another group raises the issue of "the news. . . . They show the Middle East, its deserted places . . . people running, guns, little kids, scaring and killing Americans." Another discussion led one participant to conclude that "it has to do with what your community is made up of. If you see a Middle Eastern person on TV that you don't see around your neighborhood, you think, there's a bad guy."

Participants in Arab American focus groups, though, have a different response in relation to their feelings of personal safety in relation to the media. Responding that a feeling of personal threat was not there, one informant explains that it was because "the terrorists are going to be Arabs right now, apparently, as far as the media would portray it, who wouldn't particularly care about killing me because I am Arab."

Arab American groups are much less likely to list places they would not visit, instead constructing a world relatively open for travel. However, when they do identify places to avoid, these lists center mostly on Israel and occasionally on Iraq, more specifically nations as opposed to regions. In contrast, members of other groups focus on entire regions. When questioned about one participant's response that he would not be comfortable going at all to the Middle East as a "region," another replied that he would indeed avoid "the whole region. . . . I don't know enough about the differences." Questioned further about other areas, he added that he would also avoid "Africa, eastern Europe, wherever there is some kind of conflict."

Projected maps of global space highlight different locations as causes for concern across these groups. Fear of foreign territory, for the other focus groups at least, seems intertwined with a sense of despair.

Fear of terrorist threat finds grounding in the suspenseful plots in action-adventure film. How this translates into viewers' expectations regarding danger in the global context suggests a consistent sense of fear of what becomes seen as foreign space, among some of the groups. Confessed fear of terrorism seems relatively low overall. Only 13 percent of survey respondents claimed to be anxious about potential terrorist threats, while most (65 percent) insisted they are not (22 percent were neutral; mean = 3.8 on a 5-point scale). However, separate from personal concern and consistent with third-person effects, most respondents (57 percent) do believe terrorism to be a major concern in the United States (mean = 2.5), and that the world is dangerous (51 percent, mean = 2.6).

The Arab American groups are less likely to express fear of the world and of terrorism, however, than the other groups. Participants in Arab American discussion groups are much more likely to disagree strongly that they might be anxious about potential terrorist threats (50 percent) compared with other groups (19 percent), who are more likely to agree strongly that the world is dangerous (19 percent, compared with 8 percent of Arab American groups).

For the other focus group participants, more likely to identify with their national identity as Americans, fear maps an "us versus them" construction of the world. The normative center of these discussions suggests a fear of others, and a concern that "they" don't like "us" as Americans. According to one informant, it "is a fact that other countries don't like the U.S." One focus group participant, agreeing with others that being an American overseas would be risky, suggested that if traveling one should "put a Canadian flag on your backpack." There is a recurring theme of not wanting to be identified as American outside of the United States.

Although not uniform, these groups are more likely than Arab American groups to register some fear of terrorism. For example, one explains: "Of course you have Middle East terrorists which their activities have accelerated, have been accelerating quite a bit over the years, in the past ten, twenty years maybe. . . . You have the problems with Chechnya which I guess, they're Muslim but they're not Arab, and I mean there's a lot of it going on in the world." Some believe that films helped to foster a sense of insecurity and paranoia.

When traveling in airports, most of the people in non–Arab American groups feel safe, identifying the threat as those who might be terrorists. A few do mention feeling threatened by American security officials in airports, given the "cowboy mentality out there," but this feeling is much more prevalent among Arab Americans.

This fear of traveling is considerably more prominent within discussions among the Arab American groups. Their concern is not so much with visiting particular places, but instead centers on the process of traveling, particularly in airports. Many tell long stories of what they consider embarrassing and discriminatory searches and stops in airport settings.

Stories from two different groups illustrate the anxiety felt among these informants:

> Because of my name and because I usually travel alone. Every time I go through security checkpoints I'm pretty concerned they are going to latch onto something, see something in a bag, or something like that. Not that there is anything. It's always a relief to get through. There's just this fear that there are people out there who are too stereotypical to see past the stereotype.

> I do feel anxious. When I travel overseas I'm repeatedly targeted, in multiple countries, I'm repeatedly stopped. I'm repeatedly stripped of my clothing. I'm repeatedly searched and questioned.

One common theme among these groups was the frequency with which they would be stopped going through airports. Comments such as "all the time" permeate these discussions. Another explains: "It's happened to me, it's happened to my brother, plenty of people I know. It's happened to people in Austin that I know as well. So, you have to be concerned about it."

Most believe that being selected for intensive search is indeed *not* random. The following comments characterize the tenor of these conversations: "When they say it's random that pisses me off. Stop me if you want to: you're suspicious, fine. Don't sit there and tell me it's a random search when every single person around me is flying from Lebanon or they're Indian. My Dad is used to it"; "It's not really a random search. They are looking for people, ethnic minorities, people they think are affiliated with Islam. So they'll stop me and a lot of times I feel like . . . or they'll look at your name and if it looks like an Arab name or something."

One theme that carries across focus groups is women's concerns with being harassed and assaulted given their gender, regardless of place or ethnicity. This worry further accentuates concern with being searched as an Arab woman at the airport:

> I find it annoying, like they are violating you. I just don't like being touched and everything. And they ask you to take off your belt. I feel like I'm undressing in front of the whole airport. I really don't like that, then they are touching you everywhere. I don't particularly appreciate it.

Another agrees: "I actually lost my temper: it felt like all the dirty old men watching you get patted down for the millionth time and it kind of has a setup like a mall, people are having coffee and watching me get felt up. I lost it. I had no sleep. I get stopped all the time." Her comments were met by sympathetic laughter from the group.

Several Arab American groups discuss the way that media exaggerate the threat of terrorism, in ways that benefit media industries and U.S. policies, but do not reflect actual risks encountered within or outside the United States. Fear of terrorism, according to one informant, is "being capitalized on . . . perpetuated. All of these films have some underlying theme, if not the central focus, [as] a political tool." The next participant agreed that "terrorism is . . . an issue for political gain."

In another group, an Arab American woman explained that she felt

> threatened by actually Americans more than anything. Like I personally had a lot of, um, awful things happen to me after 9/11 that could have turned a lot worse than they did. . . . It's because of the ignorance. I mean it all comes back to what we're doing. Ignorance from all the films and you know and a lot of things that happened. . . . I think I feel more threatened here even than in the Arab world. People [say]—oh, aren't you scared to go over there? I am more scared to be here [laughs] just because of the ignorance and the hate crimes.

Instead of identifying with their nationality as Americans in relation to the rest of the world, this group is more likely to identify with their affiliation as Arabs, as a code that suggests more threat within the country than outside it.

Action-Adventure Realism and Relevance

How action-adventure film figures into these perceptions of fear and terror may be articulated through participants' discussion of the potential realism and relevance of these narratives to perceptions of broader concerns with terrorism. In a scale of relevance of the genre to participants' own lives, attitudes were gauged as to the extent they agreed with statements that: action-adventure films portray realistic events (mean = 4.0 on a 5-point scale); action-adventure films portray issues relevant in my own life (mean = 3.7); and I am anxious about potential terrorist threats (mean = 3.8). Over two-thirds (69 percent) of the participants in other groups identified with the genre's relevance, compared with just over half (54 percent) of the Arab American participants (gamma = -0.32).

Consistent with expectations, those who are more exposed to this genre of film tend to be more likely to see these films as realistic and relevant. Almost half (44 percent) of those who watch many of these films see them as realistic and relevant, compared to about one-fifth (18 percent) of those who watch fewer of these films. This relationship between exposure and attitudes is strong (gamma = -0.48), particularly among the other focus groups (gamma increases to -0.57) but also among the Arab focus groups (gamma decreases to -0.43 but maintains some strength).

It appears that other groups are more likely to perceive the genre as realistic and relevant than the Arab American groups. Moreover, this sense
of personal relevance seems to be further accentuated among those who
are intensive fans of the genre. Media experiences may reinforce conditions of identity then in terms of the relative proximity the genre is expected to have in terms of other attitudes and experiences.

While other groups are more likely to be intensive fans and perceive the
relevance of the genre to their lives, the Arab American groups are much
more likely than the others to identify problems with the action-adventure genre, particularly in terms of the villains cast and the settings portrayed.

Arab American groups also point to the connection between the terrorist plots and policies of the U.S. government, a discussion lacking in the
other focus groups. As one remarks: "What is terrorism? Hollywood gives
the U.S. government point of view"; and another: "I think Hollywood has
latched on to what the media and our government call terrorism, basically
rogue groups out of the Middle East or Central America, and it used to be
Eastern Europe." Informants in several Arab American groups are quite
vocal in their critiques of U.S. political positions:

> My father comes from Iran, he was born in Iran, we have family over there,
> I lived around four years there and it's so rare that anyone who is I guess a
> natural citizen or just, you know, has grown up here would ever think to de-
> scribe an act of terrorism as like coming from America, like Americans
> couldn't do it. But my dad of course is very verbal about that, just because
> he's like, "Well, did you ever think of this?" or "Did you ever think of . . ."
> you know, America's a terrorist country too if you think about it.

> Terrorism will continue to be a serious threat to the United States . . . as long
> as we continue to have two-sided policies across the world, as long as we
> continue to move troops in and out of countries as we wish and like impose
> our sanction as well as not even going into the IMF and the World Bank.

One participant thinks it important for Arab Americans to see *The Siege*
in order to provoke recognition of how

> civil rights and the Constitution have been trampled over, in what in the
> movie is a war on terror, and I always told my Arab American friends, this is
> exactly what's going to happen to you once there is terror in the U.S. That is
> sort of exactly what happened. That's why I thought Arab Americans should
> see the movie. You realize the way your incorporation into America is always
> limited and subjected to change depending on how much power you hold.

Recognizing the links across media and U.S. foreign policy is seen as evident across news and fictional media. According to one informant:

Both of them borrow from each other quite often, and I think that what we see in movies today is like . . . our news is based on fear and it's, it sort of scares people into either adopting a certain stance or a certain policy or a certain view that maybe the administration or somebody holds in mind, and so I think that, if movies do really borrow from news, well then it's like the worst-case scenario.

Several Arab American groups point to *Three Kings* as an exception to their overarching despair with the genre as a whole:

Three Kings did a really good job showing the other side of the fence. You have these Americans and they have this goal and personal issues and these problems at home, and you have these Iraqis who have all these issues and problems and things to deal with and you can sympathize for both of them. Whether you root for whoever, that's a personal prerogative. But you can understand that these people we're fighting, these are human beings, not villains, and what they are doing, they are doing it because in some respect they think it's right. Granted, that won't make a very good action film, but that's reality in some respect.

While discussions in the other focus groups are less critical of the genre, they do share a concern with Arab American groups that villains are portrayed too simplistically and stereotypically, as discussed in the previous chapter. Their concerns with plots invoke lack of historical context and original scripts, though these discussions are much less prevalent.

MAPPING LAND AND FEAR

Interpretations of action-adventure film inform broader conceptualizations of the homeland, in which intimate and distant spaces and territories become infused with foreboding and fear. For some, this fear becomes manifest in a sense of terror emerging in foreign lands; for others, fear becomes more closely connected with particular domestic spaces and mobility. Cultural mapping of land creates boundaries through which fear of others and sense of security become articulated.

The differences across groups in cultural mapping of land are striking. In discussions of action-adventure settings, Arab American groups are much more likely than their counterparts to specify particular places over more generalized regions, and to be highly critical of rather than justify these constructions. These groups' sense of danger in the world at large, dictating concern with travel outside the known and familiar territory of citizenship, seem contingent on cultural identification as well as direct experience. The connection between identification, whether as an *American*

citizen primarily or as an *Arab* constituent, and fear in the world is critical in understanding how cultural mapping predicates experiences and
interpretations.

Fear of the world, of terrorism, and of our own country can be situated
in broader cultural climates in which the resonant narrative, in popular
culture as well as news, positions the great White American male hero
against the darker, foreign masses, exemplifying the evil that must be
vanquished. For those who identify with these heroic characterizations,
consequential mapping of the world is limited to vague senses of danger
and insularity. For those who consciously disconnect from these good-
versus-evil polarities, the sense of fear and danger is much closer to home.
Mediated memory, rooted in long-term and systemic Orientalist ideology,
permeates the cultural framing that limits our political engagement
within national as well as global discourses.

The cultural mapping articulated through action-adventure film resonates with broader interpretations of global space. Our cultural mapping
of global space embodies consequences not only to our perspectives of
communities and boundaries, but also to our sense of respect for other
cultures and of obligation to promote humanitarian justice.

The cultural landscape that becomes part of memory and knowledge
may be inspired through the familiar tropes of media, but must also be fil-
tered through the identities and experiences of viewers. Dialogue concerning the settings of action-adventure film highlights the sense of
us/United States versus them/foreign among many viewers, particularly
intensive fans. Arab American informants, though, are more likely to raise
concerns about the portrayal of the Middle East specifically, as a part of
the dangerous, foreign territory depicted in discussions among the other
viewers. This sense of insularity and lack of familiarity with the Middle
East suggest cause for concern.

The fear ascribed to particular places and spaces, perpetuated through
action-adventure narratives, calls out for heroic action. How we are expected to vanquish evil, calming these fears, is addressed in the next
chapter.

4

⁂

Conquering Evil
in Defense of Home

Home is not a mere transient shelter: its essence lies in the personalities of the people who live in it.

—H. L. Mencken (1880–1956)

This is the true nature of home—it is the place of Peace; the shelter, not only from injury, but from all terror, doubt and division.

—John Ruskin (1819–1900)

Our heroes are those . . . who . . . act above and beyond the call of duty and in so doing give definition to patriotism and elevate all of us. . . . America is the land of the free because we are the home of the brave.

—David Mahoney

The critical root of "homeland" lies in the idea of "home," evoking a sense of belonging and refuge. Within the political rhetoric of homeland security, home becomes more than a reference to a dwelling or residence, instead connoting a national community of people sheltered from harm. National heroes, dedicated to the core values of patriotic duty, are those who are believed to protect this home from external threat.

This chapter considers what we learn from action-adventure film in relation to these heroes, who are in the process of conquering evil. In the context of Hollywood-based film, the myth of American exceptionalism reigns. As Shohat and Stam (1994) skillfully demonstrate, "the cinema" becomes "ideally suited to relay the projected narratives of nations and

empires" (101). In framing his own film analysis, Rameriz-Berg (2008) emphasizes the importance of manifest destiny, justifying and sanitizing U.S.
conquest of other territories, as a central feature of action film narratives.
Dittmer's (2005) study of *Captain America* illustrates how this hero exemplifies a national ideal, as a strong, moralistic leader acting "in the name of
security, not empire" (630). Yet it is the projection of "empire" that becomes
embedded in the cinematic narrative, typically from "the colonizer's perspective" (Shohat and Stam 1994, 109). Imperial conquest becomes sub-
merged in discourses of "rescuing" those groups, often foreign women,
who are framed as being in distress and unable to help themselves.

As a manifestation of a hegemonic set of traits, U.S.-based heroes are
more likely to be White, male Christians (Dittmer 2005). These heroes assert "White superiority," as these characters radiate objectivity and expertise (Shohat and Stam 1994, 200). Arab characters are posed as devas-
tatingly evil villains, such that in contrast American heroes can radiate,
vanquishing threats to American culture (Eisele 2002). Gibson (1994) relates the myth of the lone gunman prevalent in U.S. film to a "war culture" rooted in U.S. political history. His work on the portrayal of heroes
in post-Vietnam film confirms the positioning of U.S. forces as "virtuous
defenders of a just cause" (21), who win battles on behalf of the nation. In
the process, boys mature into men and war appeals as a safe and attractive mechanism for resolving conflict. Similarly, Prince (1992) demonstrates the nationalistic spirit invoked in films, particularly during the
Reagan era, when narratives address U.S. "society under threat" (32) as
our "charismatic hero" confronts the "dehumanized villain" (195).

Inextricably linked to patriotic duty, the great American hero exemplified through action-adventure conquers evil. His violent responses are
justified as necessary given an immediately pressing situation of impend-
ing doom with moral righteousness on his side. Good and evil are clearly,
diametrically opposed. Within this context, our handsome, muscular
hero, articulated in exactly those terms by most of the research participants, is able to conquer evil, typically through his individual prowess
rather than through any sense of collective effort.

The strength of these heroes appeals to many action-adventure fans.
One Arab American informant expressed his enjoyment of

> action movies where you get into the role of the character. This individual
> is fighting the bad guys, or evil character, and that's really the plot, and
> then the special effects or action just serve to glorify the character. . . . I
> think the best action movies, the ones I like the best, are the ones where I
> most identify with the character, because, especially when I was younger,
> I'd walk around and think of myself as these action heroes, fighting these
> bad guys.

A participant in a non–Arab American focus group expressed a similar sentiment:

> I have a three-year-old son and every time he watches action-adventure, he's, that's exactly right, he looks like he feels powerful. If he's emulating *Star Wars* he gets his light saber. He's serious about it. This is work. You can tell he's completely trying to identify with whoever was on the screen. I do that too. I just love to envision myself doing those things. I want to be that girl who's doing everything perfect.

While the appeal of heroes may transcend cultural differences, a sense of identification with them differs dramatically, particularly given the dominant demographic characteristics ascribed to these characters.

THE GREAT AMERICAN HERO

The dominant descriptions of these heroes accentuate these characters as beacons of light, through the clean-shaven, blond, and blue-eyed appearance of men characterized in ways consistent with the normative center in the United States: European American, light skinned, Christian, male.

White European American

Discussions and descriptions of heroes, as well as villains, tend to conflate issues of ethnicity and nationality. In this analysis, however, I first disentangle specific reference to ethnicity, and then accord attention to nationality. It should be recognized, though, that the hero articulated through this research holds a U.S. passport and is of European descent.

When asked to describe a "typical hero" in an open-ended question, about one-third (33 percent) refers to ethnicity. Arab American groups are more likely to articulate ethnicity in their descriptions of heroes (52 percent) than the others (19 percent). Of these, each description refers explicitly to "White" or "Caucasian" features.

When detailing heroes actually seen in specific action-adventure films, however, the racial and ethnic identifications of these characters demonstrate more variation: although most describe characters specifically as White or Caucasian (64 percent), some also mention African American (27 percent) and other distinctions (9 percent). Members of Arab American groups appear to be more cognizant of ethnicity in describing specific heroes (47 percent, compared with only 9 percent among other groups), but their recognition of Caucasian and African American heroes does not differ greatly from members of other groups who produce these descriptions. There appears to be more recognition of diversity in actual films remembered than in constructions of idealized heroes.

Arab American focus groups point to the way that non-White groups tend to have their ethnic identities accentuated within films. In the following discussion, one of these groups describes how "Mexican," "Chinese," and "Black" stereotypes become pronounced:

> Ethnicities are always stressed, I think, when there's a difference. Whether it's Desperado and his Mexican ethnicity, that's going to be stressed through the whole movie. There's going to mariachi music playing, he's always going to be speaking in an accent. Same thing with kung fu movies where the Chinese hero is going to be expressing that in some way or another, what he eats, or how he speaks, or who his friends are.

> Yeah, I mean, come on, if a guy's Black, if it's Wesley Snipes when he pulls up to save the day they are playing rap music in the background and you know they are always talking, exactly. There's mariachi bands if you're Hispanic, and if you're White, nothing is stressed at all. They just play something something composed for the movie. It doesn't jump out at you. It's probably to distract you from the fact that all of them are White.

The problem of Arab characters, particularly in relation to African American characters, is stressed in several of the Arab American groups. Across two different groups, the following sets of comments illustrate the tension in appreciation of a non-White hero along with continued concern about the problematic portrayal of Arab characters.

> I have one more comment on *The Siege*. I think the movie wouldn't have been balanced if he hadn't been Black. I mean, if he was White, everybody else, in general, everybody else you see in the movie is White except the Arabs who are the terrorists. And you have Tony Shalhoub who is supposed to be Arab as well. If you didn't have him there being Black the movie would have been completely imbalanced. There wouldn't be a Black man in the movie and it would be a racially stereotyped movie. I feel he had to be Black: even though it wasn't important to his character, it was important to the movie.

> It still confounds me that in *The Siege* and in *Three Kings* there's Black protagonists, so . . . it becomes for me almost like the Black guy who is even tougher than the White guy to take on the Arabs. It's so bizarre to me, it gets back to, anytime you cast a Black person it seems you're being very liberal or multicultural or correct, but to me I think it's even more stereotyping. In my mind it's like, it takes a tougher guy to get the Arabs, or "really we're not being racist"— look, we have a Black guy beating the Arab. Or, you know, it's so bizarre, I can't understand it, but we've come so far. I don't understand, there's something going on that's more subtle.

In contrast, discussions among the other focus groups of the same film, *The Siege*, demonstrate a remarkable lack of memory of the ethnicity of certain characters. For example, an informant remarks: "I can't remember if the hero is Black or White, and I'm pretty sure he's Black. I don't remember—I remember the terrorists and the crazy White chick who had been an Arabic studies person, but I'm pretty sure the hero was Black. Do you remember?" In response, the others in this group shook their heads no, indicating that they could not remember either.

Asian American informants in these groups point to Jackie Chan as an occasionally cast hero, but "not the same sort of hero." In order for "Asian men" to be portrayed as heroes, informants believe they must be the "crafty martial arts guy or whatever" doing "karate." Memory of specific characters appears contingent on cultural identification with the actors, often named, playing heroic figures.

The non–Arab American groups posit what they perceive to be conventional wisdom about the absence of an Arab hero. One exemplary comment details that "you definitely wouldn't see, like, an Arab hero. Like, I don't think there's ever been one, probably." One set of justifications points to the commercialization of the film industry. If one wanted "to make a lot of money," one would "want to make the brothers, you know, dark skinned, dark haired, accented, very loud, typically, you know, loud voices are a trait of the Middle Eastern people. You don't stop talking, you talk over someone else." In this discussion, the group debates the utility of a potential strategy to create an Arab hero by tricking the potential film producers: "You don't make the hero Arab and you don't make the villain White. You tweak it a little bit so when you're making this pitch the people don't laugh you out of the room." Clearly an Arab hero against a White villain seems to defy normative logic on the conditions distinguishing good from evil.

Comments excerpted from another non–Arab American group illustrate an underlying concern with perceived appearance:

> I mean, you're talking about Hollywood, and I don't think we're at a time in our country right now because Arabs are so vilified that people find Arabs attractive. They see an Arab and they think that guy's Saddam Hussein.

> Not when they're labeled that way. I've seen a lot of, like, you know, Arabian, Persian, half or whatever out there and no one will say anything, like it won't be like . . . you know . . .

> They're not like reality to the society. If there was someone that went on *Am I Hot or Not* and it was an Arab, how far would that person get? An Arab male.

> That depends. Is it an ugly Arab or a pretty Arab? They're not all the same!

No, that's true.

If she takes off her veil, like what? [Laughter.]

What are you laughing for here?

I don't know . . . it just seems very . . .

I mean, it's like, "You're from Texas, where's your hat?" I mean, I'm half-Persian, where's my veil? Like it's [hums Middle Easternish tune]. You know? I don't know.

The close integration of ethnicity with other characteristics is explained by one informant: "I think it's not only ethnicity, but the entire hero niche, the niche that constitutes the hero is not only White, it's of a certain class, of a certain historicity, of a certain belief structure, a certain allegiance." The conflation of ethnicity with nationality is particularly prominent in discussions of characters from Arab cultures and Arab nations.

The identification of nationality for action-adventure heroes seems to be much simpler and less complex than that of described villains. Across the board, informants agree that the heroes seen as well as the heroes idealized are American. In open-ended descriptions in survey responses, almost one-half (48 percent) explicitly refer to "American" characters in films they had seen. Similarly, the "red-blooded American" is agreed on as "typical" of this genre of film. Arab American groups were also more likely to volunteer this description of nationality in their discussions of typical (52 percent, compared with 19 percent) heroes, though the difference was less paramount in descriptions of actual films recalled (50 percent compared with 47 percent).

Even when a film is set in another country, the narrative relies on an American hero. One informant finds it amusing that in *The Last Samurai* the hero was American: "It sort of makes me laugh because I did go see it with a bunch of friends. The movie we thought was good and everything, but still the concept of Tom Cruise being the last samurai still just makes us laugh, 'cause even though it's a movie that takes place almost entirely in Japan, the hero is still an American."

The American heroes are seen as directly connected to the state in Arab American discussions. One group explicitly connects "the White House" with heroes' characters, who typically portray "FBI agents, CIA, police officers, military men, [and others] directly linked to the U.S. government."

Other group participants assume that this constant presentation of the American hero is justified in part because of the perceived domestic audience and in part because of an assumed capacity and superiority of the United States in relation to the rest of the world. With reference to the latter assumption, one informant boasts: "We've got the money in the real world, so we usually come out on top. We pay for bigger weapons." Another group's conversation further exemplifies these sentiments:

> It seems that only Americans have the infrastructure and capacity to save the world, as if . . . the armed forces from other countries are absolutely incapable, they are just wasting their time and it's only Americans who have the brain-power and muscle power to save the day.

> That's very true, especially in that one where they are going all over the world and everyone is cheering. My studies are about Africa and what do they do. They have—of course, there are a lot of people who live in rural parts of Africa—but there are also a lot of big cities and professional people who are African too. But that wouldn't have been a typical African image to Americans—Americans definitely see people still carrying a spear.

> All the other countries seem to standing around praying. They weren't doing anything.

> [Laughter.]

Another type of justification emphasizes the domestic market within the United States as a central feature in determining the nature of the hero's characteristics. Hollywood films, it is assumed, are made for American audiences. This explanation appears to be shared across types of participants and groups. One Arab American informant explains that "Americans aren't going to relate to someone who is Russian the way they would if he was African American or Mexican American or Arab American," suggesting that ethnicity could vary even if nationality might not, and that to be "American" is to be White.

One Arab American informant offers a more critical view of the marketing assumption that the U.S. domestic audience should or does take precedence:

> You know what bothers me, these are always marketed towards the world and I think the world just accepts the fact there's going to be a White American hero in every movie. It's not even up for scrutiny; it's just accepted. I think the same goes with me. Where I live in a culture where you never have as many people in the media, you just accept that's the way it is. You move past that point. You don't scrutinize it. That's what the hero is going to be. Kids all over the world identify with these action heroes even though they're not White themselves.

The assumptions guiding justifications for the features attributed to the hero's ethnicity and nationality find similar currents when considering his religious or spiritual affiliation. The normative center of patriotism to the homeland overshadows potential variation in characteristics.

The Christian/Secular Undercurrent

Heroes within U.S. action-adventure film accentuate the attributes of the idealized "home," in this case based in Christian or secular communities. These characteristics, though, are described less frequently than those of ethnicity or nationality. Moreover, discussions of heroes' religious affiliations are remarkably shorter than those of the villains'. Most informants neither remember a particular religion in connection with heroes actually seen in films nor suggest a religious affiliation of a typical hero. The very few who do (8 percent of Arab American and 3 percent of other groups) indicate religious affiliation in survey answers agree: Christian.

Arab American discussions of this feature, when prompted in focus group discussions, profess an assumption that heroes are specifically Protestant by default. As one explains: "As far as religion, like, a lot of the movies I can think of, the hero's religion almost never comes into play. But the villains' do." As the group nodded in agreement, another chimed in: "It's like if religion is going to come into play I feel like it's always with the villain. It's like the hero's religion doesn't. . . . And then you always just assume that they're, if you know they're White and American then it's probably Christian or something."

The only informant to recall a central positive Muslim character describes the role played by Morgan Freeman in *Robin Hood*:

> It was like the Moor, and he was, like, supposed to be very rational as the Muslim. All the gringos are beating each other up in Britain, and it's kind of coming from Spain as it's transferring over and he prays religiously—regularly in the direction of Mecca—and he's rational and cleaner. It's trying to throw that stereotype a little on edge, or trying to show what the UK looked like at that time, so that was a little bit of a switch. I always assume that the whiteys are kind of areligious. I think it's the idea of God in the U.S., but they certainly don't go to church or pray.

While none of the other focus groups explicitly recognize a positive Muslim character, there are differences of opinion as to whether there was ever a Jewish hero. One self-identified Jewish participant claims there is not, while in another group someone describes a dialogue in which one of the characters in *Independence Day* identifies himself as Jewish.

When pressed to identify a religious connection to heroes' characters, some identify a "generic American Christian or whatever," and as another explains, "it's a statistical likelihood." One informant describing the character played by Tony Shalhoub in *The Siege* has trouble recalling: "One of the guys on the team is Islamic, or he might not even be Islamic, just Arabic." The conflation of Islam with Arab identity seems rarely questioned in these discussions with non–Arab American viewers.

Some of these informants felt uncomfortable expressing religious affiliation at all. For example, when asked to describe more fully an idealized Palestinian character in a theoretical film, one participant paused, and then responded: "Gosh, I feel like such an, I don't know, I'm falling into the trap."

In these other groups, unlike the Arab American groups, many express the sentiment that heroes do not have any religious affiliation. "A lot of times they are so tough, they shake off religion. They are very independent-type figures." Religion, it was suggested, would be "too deep" or complex for this genre, and might alienate the audience.

Invisibility of dominant culture appears quite striking in these discussions of religion. Among other focus groups, the assumption that heroes are secular reigns, while among the Arab American groups, the presumption of Christianity seems to arise as the normative default. With each group, the markers of spiritual belief or lack thereof are implicit, not typically marked in obvious ways they recall in discussions of specific films.

The Macho Mainstream

Similar to discussions of ethnicity, nationality, and religion, the "typical" hero is overwhelmingly agreed on as male, while recognition of women as well as men is evident in discussions of films actually seen. In open-ended descriptions of "typical heroes," over one-third (39 percent) explicitly mention male as a central attribute (more likely to be mentioned among Arab American groups, 44 percent, than other group, 36 percent participants.) In the other survey question concerning descriptions of films seen, about 5 percent describe female heroes, but the overwhelming majority of participants, across groups, explicitly recognize heroes as male.

In this instance there appears to be consistency across Arab American and other groups. The White American male embodies the quintessential action-adventure hero, while women are recognized as leveraging their resources through sexual power rather than through physical or intellectual strength. One participant remarks: "Women are expected to do all these things men have to do, but we're supposed to do it with a lot less clothing." This is a concern for women across groups: "I would like to see women heroes or villains that are not using their sexuality as a tool."

Similar to a justification for heroes being American, many argue that action-adventure heroes should be male because these "films are watched by males" so "are catering to this audience." Others just argue that this is the way it is: "When I think of a hero I'll probably think of a male just because it's the way things have been."

Some note that American women are seen as less likely to "carry a gun. But this 'other' from this foreign place will kick your head off." Moreover, when women do act in heroic roles, they "internalize the power structure they are in. Like, for example, a huge thing I have with *GI Jane* is, it's supposed to be this woman as the hero and that's really good because you don't usually see that but by the same token she does that by going into the military and internalizing military values and becoming masculine in that way."

Across groups, women describe their wish to assert female heroes, particularly as "independent" and not supplementary to central male figures. One woman aspires to see a female hero who "stands alone, and doesn't need anybody at all ever. She [would be] capable of doing [things] on her own and she does not fall apart and need to call this guy, or anything like that. Typically the way women are portrayed when she does get the gun away from the criminal, he [the hero] just wrenches it out of her wrist anyway. Can we avoid that? Let her be a hero and independent."

Female actresses recalled during these discussions include Nicole Kidman and Jennifer Garner. Even these well-known actresses played roles more supplemental than elemental to these plots, though. For example, in "*The Peacemaker*, Nicole Kidman was like the scientist, the brains, the hero, but she still had to have George Clooney there, who was a big army guy. They ran around together. It was nice to throw in this feisty female character but she still had to have a guy running around with her." Similarly, "in *Daredevil*, Jennifer Garner is real feisty and fights and kills everybody but that's like, in a comic book. Even in *The Peacemaker*, Nicole Kidman for the first half of the movie is wearing a skirt and high heels." One Arab American woman vaguely remembered "a female of Middle East descent and she was helping the hero."

While the male heroes may be assisted by attractive female companions in many of these films, in the end, they work alone. The projection of individual achievement within U.S. culture finds grounding in projected parameters of masculinity.

The Lone Hero

Consonant with Northern, Western ideologies, the notion of the lone hero (Gibson 1994) permeates action-adventure narratives at the expense of portraying more collective efforts. This characterization of conquering evil resounds across groups. One informant would prefer to see

> a group effort. Like I've seen a few movies where it's like a group of people saving the day, and you have different kinds of people that are like playing different roles and having a group dynamic and stuff like that and I think that's the way it works more in real life. You're not saved by one courageous FBI agent, you're saved by a group of FBI agents working together with the CIA agents sharing information, and with the local police, and everybody

shares information and works together. But then you can have a diversity of heroes, 'cause then everyone can find the hero they can identify with the most.

In response to the above statement, participants engaged in the following dialogue:

Like *Scooby Doo*.

Exactly!

Scooby Doo is a hero.

Yeah, well, a group effort.

Heroes are indeed so individualist that viewers often conflate names of actors with names of characters, similar to discussions of evidence described in Jhally and Lewis's (1992) research on *The Cosby Show*. Also, unlike in discussions of villains, informants are much more likely to remember names of actors playing heroes. The most commonly described actors corresponding with the most frequently mentioned action-adventure films include Arnold Schwarzenegger, Denzel Washington, Bruce Willis, Keanu Reeves, and Harrison Ford (listed in order of how frequently they were mentioned in focus groups). While Schwarzenegger, Willis, and Ford serve as illustrations of the exemplary White, male, American hero, Washington exemplifies the African American who has been able to break through the typical mold, and Reeves the multicultural actor claimed by several groups as their own (Park, forthcoming). As one informant summarizes: "You have a lot of White men, you have your Bruce Willis, you have your Harrison Ford, you have your Arnold Schwarzenegger, then you have your Black heroes like your Denzel Washington and your Will Smith and whatnot."

Schwarzenegger is by far described more frequently than any other actor in discussions of action-adventure heroes. In *True Lies*, Arnold Schwarzenegger plays the central hero, Harry Tasker, as a European American agent with a German accent. Informants refer to him consistently by his real and not character name. Although this film includes other heroes, such as Jamie Lee Curtis as his wife, Tom Arnold as his friend, and other government agents, including European and Arab men and women, informants do not mention these characters or actors in their descriptions or discussions. Described as "a badass hero," Schwarzenegger's characters are noted for single-handedly taking on "the entire militia." Discussions of his nationality, as a person and as a character, demonstrate the willingness of viewers to accommodate Schwarzenegger into the American fold. Several participants explain that even though they believed that Schwarzenegger was "not even American," and as another remarked "Austrian . . . [and] has this accent," they believe "most people would consider him an American hero." Discussions point out ways "you're made to believe that he's American," such as, according to another group, "holding an American flag coffee mug and all this stuff."

Bruce Willis and Harrison Ford characterize the quintessential American hero much more easily, with less lengthy explanation than the others. Playing the U.S. president in *Air Force One*, Harrison Ford overshadows the heroic actions of the others, including Glenn Close playing the role of the vice president. In discussions of this film, most participants focus on his status as an actor or his role as president, with just two people mentioning his Caucasian ethnicity. In these discussions, Harrison Ford is described as a "normal guy" or a "regular guy," within the other focus groups, whereas participants in an Arab American group want to be clear that their pronouncement of Ford as able to "kick terrorists' asses" is "sarcastic." But as another participant laughingly remarks, he "can't see Bush doing the things that Harrison Ford did *at all*."

Similar to the normative European American male hero representing political authority, Bruce Willis portrays a police officer in *Die Hard*. In descriptions of this film, most emphasize Bruce Willis as an actor, and about half consider his character's professional status as a police officer. Other heroes, such as the African American police officer Sergeant Powell (played by Reginald Veljohnson), are not mentioned in these discussions. Bruce Willis is described as "witty," "believable," in his heroic characters, though in one discussion within an Arab American group their collective idealized version of a new action-adventure film features Bruce Willis as a villain, dying in the end (a concept met with much laughter within the group), avenged by heroic Muslim women.

When asked questions regarding the ethnicity of heroes, most participants tend to reply "White," unless the hero is played by Denzel Washington. Some of the other African American actors mentioned include Will Smith, Samuel Jackson, and Wesley Snipes. Most of the other focus groups stress Denzel Washington as a popular, "good-looking," "cute" African American actor, generally well liked by viewers, with only a few exceptions: one calling him a "puss face" and another "the token Black guy." Playing a political authority in *The Siege* similar in style to those of Bruce Willis and Harrison Ford, Denzel Washington represents an African American male FBI agent. More so than in descriptions of heroes in other films, informants describing this film are more likely to include specific mentions of Washington's ethnicity, or that of another secondary heroic figure played by Tony Shalhoub.

Proportionately many fewer Arab American groups discuss Denzel Washington, and when they do, they are more critical. Instead of seeing him as contributing to a more racially diverse set of American heroes, Arab American discussions exhibit a more complicated sense of the racial identity of his characters. In one instance, a participant explains that

> with *The Siege*, I didn't feel like they stressed Denzel Washington being Black. It didn't seem to be a factor at all. He could have been White. It wasn't, it didn't seem to be a factor in the movie at all. He just doing a job, he was kicking ass: that was his function. He was Black, he was, I guess, the hero, but it didn't seem to matter that he was Black.

Instead of having this actor play a character in ways that function very similarly to the typical White American male hero, these informants would prefer to see other potential attributes highlighted. When one informant suggests that "it would have been interesting if Denzel Washington was a Black Muslim," another responds: "That would have been too complicated," to the sounds of laughter.

Finally, Keanu Reeves signifies a more complex actor in the eyes of these viewers, discussed more frequently among Arab American than other focus groups. Reeves represents a variety of ethnicities and nationalities as a Canadian citizen born in Lebanon with Chinese, Hawaiian, and English heritage. When one informant explains that "Keanu Reeves was born in Beirut, but I mean, nobody knows that," the immediate response within that group is:

> But he doesn't look stereotypically American. . . . I know my stereotype would be the blond-haired, blue-eyed, 5'8", 5'9", I mean, decently built with a beer belly or something, that's my idea of an American. . . . That's a stereotype they have outside of the U.S. They think they're all blond and blue eyed; they're not.

The only informant in a non–Arab American group to discuss this actor identifies himself as "Chinese," affiliating Reeves with Asian cultures: "I would have Chinese friends try to claim the Chinese blood in Keanu Reeves, and I would have Korean friends trying to say he's part Korean." This actor tends to be identified by and popular among Arab Americans and other non-White Americans, compared with other research informants.

In discussions of *Speed* specifically, Keanu Reeves's ethnicity as Officer Jack Traven is largely unremarked on. Only one informant describes him as "White." As in discussions of other films, participants mostly refer to the actor's name or role as a police officer, largely ignoring other central heroic figures, such as Sandra Bullock as Reeves's female counterpart.

Similarly, discussions of Ben Affleck as Jake Ryan, a CIA agent, tend to focus on Affleck specifically, in terms of his status as an actor or professional role within the film, mostly ignoring other central characters (such as Morgan Freeman) as well as Affleck's ethnicity. Only one informant mentions ethnicity, referring to Ryan as the "White guy." Knowledge of Affleck's character's name and his occupation likely may also be affected by an industry focusing attention on the Jack Ryan character narrated in several books by Tom Clancy and played by Alec Baldwin (*The Hunt for Red October*) and Harrison Ford (*Patriot Games* and *Clear and Present Danger*) in other films.

CONQUERING EVIL

The contrast between the articulation of settings, heroes, and villains in film texts and viewers' memories of these features highlights some critical concerns. First, audience memory works quite differently in terms of heroes versus villains. Informants appear more likely to recall the names of actors playing heroes than of those playing villains, and indeed to refer to the characters more by the actors' than the characters' names at all. More specificity is recalled of heroes than of villains, such as their professional position, perhaps in part attributable to the featured individualist nature of the hero as opposed to many of the villains being presented in anonymous larger groups.

Memory of the ethnicity of characters is more prominent in discussions of some films than others. When heroes are not uniformly White, as in *The Siege*, their ethnicity is more likely to be recalled and articulated. Similarly, non-White and non-American villains in *Die Hard*, *The Siege*, and *True Lies* are remembered in terms of their ethnicity and nationality. Religious affiliation, particularly Islam, is explicitly raised in terms of villains more than in terms of heroes, who are typically assumed to be Christian by Arab American groups and secular by the others. While the nationality of the hero tends to be assumed to be American, the nationalities of villains are more clearly articulated as foreign.

The perceived threat of villainous characters and exotic landscapes legitimates a need to vanquish evil through the acts of heroes identified with the dominant attributes of the homeland. Yet this sense of legitimacy, ascribed to the acts of fictitious characters as well as national policies, is not uniformly shared. Arab American groups are much less supportive of U.S. foreign policy than their counterparts. For example, when asked in the introductory survey whether U.S. military intervention in Iraq was justified, most informants disagree: Arab Americans are more adamant in the strength of their disagreement, though (mean = 4.6 on 5-point scale;

with 68 percent strongly disagreeing) than the others (mean = 4.3, with 53 percent in same category). Even though the issue of U.S. foreign aid more generally seems quite distinct from military intervention, the pattern of Arab American tendency toward less intervention in comparison to that of the others was repeated. Others are more likely to agree strongly with the statement that the United States should support foreign aid programs (39 percent, mean = 1.8) than those in Arab American groups (24 percent, mean = 2.2).

For those who identify primarily with the nation-state, as Americans first, the dominant attributes of the homeland, in terms of ethnicity, gender, and religious affiliation particularly, characterize those believed to have the capacity and the justification to use force in vanquishing evil. For those who feel less aligned with this national affiliation and more subject to a sense of Arab identity, the assertion of U.S. force, in the form of official administrative intervention as well as solo heroic efforts of the revered muscular White male, becomes much more problematic. The use of violence and force requires a belief that other forms of coercion or persuasion are not appropriate to a given situation, whether because the other party is believed to be incapable of resolving conflict through other means or the situation is believed to require immediate resolution. The action-adventure narrative creates a sense of crisis supporting the need for the latter. Prejudice against "others," particularly Arabs, distant from the normative cultural center sustains the former belief. If critical questions are not raised regarding the appropriateness and utility of violent resolution, then this assertion of force will continue to dominate our ideological consciousness as a necessary means toward preserving the homeland.

5

Re-visioning Arab Communities in U.S. Popular Culture

Action-adventure film reinscribes the narrative of terrorism within our collective consciousness, all the more poignant given its resonance with U.S. foreign policy and Orientalist ideology articulated in the nation's popular culture and news media. What we learn from these films accentuates our fear, as the sanctity of the home, aligned with the geopolitical nation-state positioned within a global context, becomes threatened by an exogenous evil personified through the villain. Some of us learn to believe that these suspenseful scenarios and villainous characters are realistic and able to be vanquished by the patriotically motivated yet individually engaged hero. Others resist this dominant characterization, asserting concern with the over simplified plots, the muted monotones of the projected landscapes, and even more problematic, the demonization of marginalized communities through their projection as villain, in stark juxtaposition to the righteous White American male hero. Viewers' very primary identification, as American or as Arab, contributes as well to their divergent senses of fear, whether directed toward foreign places representing destination of travel or toward domestic spaces, such as airports, signifying the process of travel.

Yet although we recognize the divergent interpretations and responses to action-adventure, the power to tell the story, so powerfully reinforced through an Orientalist lens, warrants serious scrutiny. Orientalist ideology comes into play when action-adventure film viewers recognize and recall Arab or Muslim features of villains, even when not present, when having a difficult time conceiving of the possibility of an Arab hero, and when asserting a realistic tone to over simplified settings and plots. For those who are ardent fans of the genre, fundamental knowledge of the political history of the Middle East appears to be lacking, along with sensitivity to prejudicial attitudes toward Arab and Muslim communities. Instead, there seems to be an unquestioning acceptance of U.S. foreign policy, legitimizing the use of violence as an appropriate means toward resolving conflict and the United States as the primary arbiter of global negotiation.

Not unlike other registered concerns with the representation of particular communities in U.S. media, Arab American viewers are much more resistant and critical of particular action-adventure films, often arguing against those who assert that the limitations of the genre itself preclude more nuanced and complex character and plot developments. The concern with media representation is shared across a variety of groups marginalized from the center of power within the United States, including those advocating improved portrayals of ethnicity, drawing attention to African American, Asian American, Latino, and Native American communities; of gender and sexuality, recognizing more complex distinctions than the dominant heteronormative and dichotomous gender roles would allow; of class, reminding us of the presence of working- and lower-class conditions; and of religious affiliation, illustrating a diversity of faith and spiritual allegiances. Similar to the concerns raised with the characterization of oppressed groups within the United States, media may also be critiqued for limited and negative portrayals of foreign communities, particularly those from neither European nor wealthy contexts. An oft-used and unduly problematic framing used to perpetuate this hierarchical dichotomy positions "modern" cultures as superior to "traditional" mores, asserting a self-righteous character to those communities with cultural proximity. Although there have been some critical transitions in media representation, particularly in the promotion of positive roles for certain ethnic groups, for women, and for gay and lesbian groups, advocacy still has a critical place in working to improve problematic characterizations.

In some senses, how other groups have protested and attempted to change media representation may be relevant to considering how to move beyond the prescribed genre limitations toward more comprehensive and sympathetic portrayals of Arab communities. However, the particular conditions of this community need to be recognized within this discussion, given the post-9/11 discriminatory climate within the country as well as the geopolitical dynamics of the United States in relation to the Arab world. Despite their relative economic strength combined with the nation's strategic political and economic interests in the Arab region, Arab Americans' potential political power seems highly constrained by the weight of dominant prejudicial attitudes normatively accepted rather than questioned. The problem of media is paramount in this situation, as we are inundated with the Arab villain and terrorist through our popular culture, further reinforced through news media.

STRATEGIES FOR CHANGE

We know that media characterize Arab communities in particularly limited and problematic ways, and that these images have consequences. We need to do more than register concern; we need to suggest and enact change. To that end, we might consider strategies for resistance, ranging from those that would activate points of leverage by working within media industries, those that work through collective efforts against industry practice, and those that engage media production and distribution in parallel to the mainstream media industry.

Determining an appropriate strategy for change relies on a particular understanding of the nature of the problem. If we believe that the problem rests with the individual media professionals' not being knowledgeable about or sensitive to Arab communities, then a strategic educational strategy might be considered. If instead we believe that the problem lies in a lack of voice, or of indigenous narrative, then sponsoring fellowships and supporting hiring of Arab Americans as journalists or media professionals should be advocated. But these concerns are not so easily disentangled. There are a variety of issues at the root of this problem, not only in terms of the demographics or expertise of media professionals, but even more so within the organizational processes of production, expectations within genre, economic structures of the industry, political framework in terms of domestic as well as foreign policies, and underlying ideological climate of Orientalism. Each one of these concerns implies a different set of potential strategies and goals, as well as potential for immediate and sustained change. The degree to which these more structural and ideological forces weigh heavily constricts the possibility for communication to become an appropriate or effective solution.

In order to consider the possibility for change, we will review potential strategies. First, approaching change through working within the industry is considered, such as enhancing the expertise of media professionals, supporting the inclusion of Arab voice, employing consultants, and working within a variety of genres to resist stereotypes.

Working within the Industry

Strategies that attempt to work within the industry tend to relegate more structural concerns to the margins, emphasizing the potential for constructive engagement within existing media organizations. Advocates working in this realm might attempt to work directly with media professionals, to promote particular constituencies or those sympathetic to these issues as future media professionals, or work as consultants in media production. Understanding the relative constraints and possibilities presented as inherent within particular genres and formats might also facilitate attempts at shifting problematic portrayals within media.

Media Professionals

At the level of media professionals, one might work to enhance the knowledge and sensitivity of writers, directors, producers, journalists, and others involved in creative production. Many may already be actively seeking expertise and experience with Arab communities in the Middle East. Others may be interested in learning more, either for the sake of a particular project or in the pursuit of more humanitarian ideals. Building in a structural reward system for these professionals might allow positive incentives to foster change within the industry.

There are several organizations rewarding media professionals for their support of designated ideals or their sympathetic portrayals of particular communities. In one example, the Harvard School for Public Health sponsored the Designated Driver Campaign. Building on their encouragement to include characters explicitly describing themselves as designated drivers, they host annual ceremonies offering rewards to individual media professionals (Singhal and Rogers 1999). Given these circumstances, media professionals then might consider the positive incentives offered through institutional rewards and public prestige against potential concerns with unwanted critique or controversy.

On an individual level, fellowships, internships, and scholarships might help support Arab Americans in their education and professional integration into media industries. In addition to working with currently employed media professionals, another strategy would consider supporting future media professionals either directly representing Arab and Arab American communities or representing at least those sympathetic to their concerns. Other strategies might help promote community media production, through subsidizing cameras and other equipment, as well as teach media literacy.

Recognizing the work of Arab American creative professionals should also help to accentuate existing talent within the industry. Acknowledging Arab heritage of celebrities may strengthen the legitimacy of this cultural community in public discourse. The status of celebrated stars with Arab ancestry, such as Salma Hayek, Shakira, Paul Anka, Alan Alda, Jamie Farr, Danny Thomas, Vic Tayback, and others, could be used to leverage cultural prestige. It is worth noting the explicit advocacy of artists, such as composer Halim El-Dabh, DJ Khaled, actress Kathy Najimy, actor Tony Shalhoub, and journalist Anthony Shadid. When established celebrities take a stand on these stereotypes, we have the benefit of immediate media attention as well as the established credibility of the individual star. When Casey Kasem, a host of U.S. radio programs and voice actor of Lebanese descent, left his audio work with the *Transformers* series, he explicitly connected his departure with his concerns over the villainous portrayals of cartoon Arabs (Kasem 1990, 6). Celebrating the professional as well as political accomplishments of these stars through the auspices of Arab American organizations such as the American Arab Discrimination Committee (ADC) may contribute to strategic efforts to change the discriminatory climate perpetuated through limited media characterizations.

Asserting an Arab voice should not be confused, however, with a projection of homogeneity, particularly critical given the tendency in the news for projected Arab perspectives to be articulated or obscured by American, Israeli, or other non-Arab sources. The confusion becomes even more pronounced when Arab sources in news and information programs are expected to explain Islam, when often these informants, such as James Zogby and the late Edward Said, are Christian. The expectation that one voice could represent such an incredibly diverse community within a national, regional, or global context illustrates the severe limitations of our comprehension. Yet we continue to expect individual media artists from more marginalized groups to illustrate the character of their entire communities.

Although one voice should not be expected to represent the diversity within any cultural community, supporting the articulation of an indigenous perspective through advocating the training and hiring of media professionals with relevant backgrounds may serve to bring sensitivity to media productions. Arab American media artists and professionals might offer more complexity to the characters as well as the context of the action-adventure narrative.

While individual creative professionals may be expected to articulate a voice identified with their cultural community, another path may be to enhance this voice through media production centered in that community more broadly. Al Jazeera illustrates an instance of this potential, as an organization geographically located and professionally staffed mostly by constituents of Arab communities. However, consistent with the divergent responses to this station within Arab communities, neither one station nor one media professional can adequately capture Arabs' diverse perspectives and interests. To respect this very issue of diversity within a cultural community, an appropriate strategy might entail supporting several professionals and organizations rather than channeling resources unilaterally. Supporting scholarships and fellowships for creative work

and academic preparation among Arab American as well as Arab students, artists, writers, journalists, and other media professionals might
help to facilitate a broadly sympathetic yet also more nuanced characterization of Arab communities.

Consultants

While funding fellowships addresses the potential for future media professionals, other strategies need to consider more immediate means for
addressing change. Encouraging media organizations to hire consultants
in the process of production offers one way for advocacy groups to voice
their concerns before the media product becomes finalized. When invited
to comment, consultants can offer valuable information about the cultural
contexts relevant to the plot and characters, and draw attention to scenes
and language that might offend audiences. The ultimate control over the
production, however, eludes the consultant. The power of the consultant
is limited to voice, with the authority for change remaining within the industry. The potential success of this consultation process becomes contingent on the permeability of the media text, the interest of the media professionals, the approach of the consultant, and the issues at stake.

One of the most prominent consultants on Arab issues within television
and film is Jack Shaheen, academic and advocate concerned with limited
media representations of Arab communities (1984, 2001). Through the
American Arab Anti-Discrimination Committee (ADC), Shaheen and others have been able to draw attention to more beneficial portrayals, such as
those in *Three Kings*, as well as more problematic characterizations, such
as the lyrics and characters in the Disney animated film *Aladdin*. In response to the protests organized by ADC and others, film lyrics depicting
the mutilation of Arabs were changed, addressing one particular instance
of racist portrayals but not the broader issues concerning the nature of the
characters (such as the differentiating skin tones between good and evil
roles) and the landscape (accentuating an exotic and distant vision of
deserts and camels; Wingfield and Karaman 2000). As a potential resolution, ADC advocated the hiring of consultants to work with media professionals in the process of film production. With the more recent experience of consultants working on the production of *The Kingdom*, results
were again mixed, with a hired consultant claiming that the script had
been improved over a previously worse one, arguing against advocates
criticizing the typically virtuous Americans fighting against the treacher-
ous Muslims (Abou-Alsamh 2007; Shaheen 2007).

In considering the potential utility of consultation as a strategy, it is
worth exploring *The Siege* as an illustration. Lawrence Wright (2004),
screenwriter for this film, has raised several concerns about how this par-

ticular consultation process worked. Having lived and worked in Cairo, Wright was prepared to create a script that captured anxiety about terrorism in the United States while provoking critical concerns with civil liberties, yet in a way that he felt would be sympathetic to Arab communities. By recommending Tony Shalhoub to play the role of the Arab American FBI agent, Wright felt that this character would offer a balanced contrast to the other Arab villains.

During the production process, several organizations and individuals were consulted, including ADC, CAIR, and Jack Shaheen. Some scenes were changed in response to this consultation, including one of an argument with a taxi driver. Shaheen suggested that the villains in this film not be Arab, which was met with resistance for a variety of reasons. First, the media professionals felt that obscuring any cultural affiliation of the villains would make these characters less identifiable and recognizable, in a way that might detract from the perceived quality or realism of the narrative. Wright (2004) related events occurring in 1998 as the film's trailers were released, such as the deadly bombings in Kenya, Tanzania, and South Africa, to his perceived realism connecting Islam with acts of terror. He remains concerned that the Planet Hollywood explosions in Cape Town particularly were attributed to Bruce Willis's connection to the restaurant as well as the film. Another central issue raised by academics and advocates raises the concern that replacing Arab villains with other specified ethnic or foreign villains transfers the problem in an irresponsible manner.

Given the experience described in the production of *The Siege*, it is worth recognizing the potential for consultation to affect the text in limited ways, such as the cutting of scenes, as well as the limitations of this process, in not resolving the fundamental tension with the projection of Arabs as villains. In the end, neither camp was pleased with the outcome of this consultation. From the perspective of the advocates, the film was not altered enough to address the more critical substance of their identified concerns. From the perspective of the media professionals, they had engaged in this consultation process yet faced serious critique and resistance anyway. The concerns raised through this consultation transpired into other advocacy efforts working against the industry, discussed in the next section.

Genres

One of the central justifications given by industry representatives in response to advocates' concerns with *The Siege* pointed to what they described as the conventions of genre. The expectation that a particular genre somehow limits the possibilities for resistant narratives or contrary-to-expectation characters is guided by a sense of industry as well as audience expectation, constrained by the economic parameters of the industry. The economic incentive to replicate seemingly successful patterns indicated through genre remains paramount over offering potentially resistant characters or unconventional plots. While the conventions of action-adventure may indeed be somewhat limiting, there may be other formats, such as comedy or music, with relatively more potential.

The tenets of writing an action-adventure script are spelled out in two recent texts on the subject (Hicks 2002; Martell 2000). Hicks explains the "expectations of genre" for "action-adventure" as building on a narrative in which the "main character knowingly undertakes an impossible mission to save a society from a state of siege, and willingly faces death to defend a personal code of honor that the society shares as a value" (2002, 17). While both hero and villain are willing to sacrifice their lives for their ideals, the difference between them is the constructed morality of their characters. While the heroic protagonist typically possesses great strength and resources, along with the legitimate and moral authority often associated with an affiliation with the U.S. government, the villainous antagonist embodies a personified face to an otherwise amorphously complex and intelligent evil force. The villains, according to these authorities, need to be fully developed characters with comprehensible rationale for committing violent acts, given that "the most important element of the action film is the villain's plan" (Martell 2000, 15). The importance of perspective is clear, given Martell's observation that "every villain would be a hero if the story were told from his point of view" (2000, 19).

The suspense of the action-adventure plot may also need to build on some expectation that portrayed situations are realistic. Yet this sense of the projected reality of the text remains contingent on the experiences and expectations of the viewers, interpreted quite differently across communities. The possibility of situating the narratives within more well-developed historical and political contexts might not only enhance the potential to project realism among the more maligned groups, but also might help to educate avid action-adventure fans, offering a suggested rationale for the villain's actions.

The action-adventure genre of film implies an intriguing juxtaposition between the embedded ideology of the characters and the economic distribution of these films. While the tenets of individualism infiltrate the composition of the central heroic figures positioning the genre staunchly within an American cultural context, action-adventure also has been cited as the "the most popular export of American movies, capable of drawing enormous audiences worldwide across many differing societies, ethnicities, and languages" (Martell 2000, 27). Despite the broad distribution across cultural contexts, the action-adventure film narrative seems to be more ensconced in dominant American ideology than able to permit resistant and alternative perspectives.

Other genres and formats might allow for more flexibility in the projection of diverse characterizations, particularly when individual creators have more control over the production of the media text. Writers of music and of comedy, for example, may be less susceptible to broadscale revisions through the industry production process than writers for television and film. However, in order to appeal to a broad American audience, Arab American comedians may be playing on and reinforcing stereotypes of Arab culture, rather than resisting them. Similarly, Arab musicians working or distributing their work within the United States may be just as likely to engage in "fusion," assimilating their styles, as in resistance, such as that of the Palestinian hip-hop artist Iron Sheik. While these genres have the potential to offer avenues for resistant voices, comedy and music can just as easily parody as empower, depending on the artist, the audience, and the conditions of production and reception.

Working within and resisting the limitations of genre, and with attempting to promote Arab voices and others respectful of Arab communities, represent some of the strategies that might be invoked in working within the media industry. These strategies are limited, however, by the economic structure of the media industry, encouraging the replication of conventional narratives in order to facilitate financial profit. If one believes that the political-economic structure of the industry or the ideological climate transcends the ability of solitary consultants or professionals, then working against or separately from the industry might be worth considering.

Working against the Industry

Recognizing the limitations of attempting to foster change within organizations, some strategies attempt to compel change through external means. Organizations advocating the interests of particular communities may attempt to raise awareness of problematic stereotypes and to convince media professionals to change their practices through strategic protests using a variety of means. These strategies might attempt to reward the industry through outside recognition for sympathetic portrayals as illustrated in the previous section, or to punish limited and problematic characterizations, addressed in this section.

Working against the industry builds on collective strategies initiated through social movement organizations, able to mobilize constituents and to channel resources. Concerned with broader social discrimination and prejudice, organizations representing constituencies of ethnicity, sexuality, religion, and other markers of identity may incorporate attention to

media within a broader array of strategies. Their attention to media recognizes the potential of popular culture as well as news in contributing to
normative climates perpetuating inequalities.

As a particularly well-organized and active group, the National Association for the Advancement of Colored People (NAACP) has been able to
leverage political clout in Hollywood in part as a consequence of its access to congressional caucuses in Washington, D.C. and in part as an ex-
tension of a relatively unified voice, particularly in comparison with the
several groups advocating on behalf of Latino communities in addressing
media industries (Downing and Beltran 2002). Whereas there may be too
many diverse organizations advocating Latino concerns, the Asian American and Native American communities may be suffering from too few,
with much less political leverage than the NAACP. In this situation, coali-
tions may help to coordinate broader support for issues similar in substance and relevant across a variety of constituencies (Downing 2004). In
response to the efforts of the Multi-Ethnic Coalition, the television industry appointed vice presidents to represent diverse communities, but most
of these posts were staffed by African Americans, illustrating the promi-
nence of the NAACP in this process. Moreover, while in some instances
persons serving in these positions were quite actively engaged in promoting substantive change (notably Disney/ABC and Fox, Downing
2004), in most cases these agents were more ornamental than integral.

Another consideration for advocacy organizations concerns the nature
of the message articulated. The more resonant the projected issue may be
with dominant cultural themes (Gamson 1988), the more potentially viable the ideas may be as a sympathetic cause within public discourse. In
addition, the more moderate the message, particularly in relation to competing controversial stances branching from similar concerns, the more
potentially attractive as a popular cause. Although Dr. Martin Luther
King expressed a variety of concerns, from those articulated in the opti-
mistic and idealistic "I have a dream" speech to other clearly critical remarks about the U.S. government, over time his work has been painted as
the more conciliatory of the spokespersons advocating for the rights of
African Americans, in direct contrast to the adversarial voice of Malcolm
X. The selected messages from Martin Luther King may have seemed
more palatable to White Middle Americans in contrast with those from
Malcolm X, and the concerns of the National Organization of Women
more so than other more radical feminist movements (Barker-Plummer
1995). Having several groups and voices representing a community may
benefit the overarching cause as combined multiple efforts outweigh the
potential of one organization.

As an illustration of a successful boycott strategy, La Raza was able to
achieve some improvement concerning the representation of Latino com-

munities in media, following the publication of its commissioned report highlighting minimal presence (Downing and Beltran 2002). More recently, groups organized to protest the exclusion of Latino and Latina contributions to World War II in Ken Burns's PBS documentary on the subject.

Another case in which collective action successfully achieved a central shift in visual representation of Latino and Asian communities can be found in protests of a Minneapolis restaurant's (Chino Latino) advertisements (Shah 2004). Some of the offending billboards include statements such as: "Happy Hour, Cheaper than a Bangkok Brothel" and "Everything but Dog." Latino and Asian American groups in Minneapolis formed a coalition to protest through a variety of acts, including writing letters, performing street theater, advocating boycotts, and securing signatures on petitions. While the groups were successful in having these advertisements taken down, they were not able to convince restaurant managers to change offensive verbal references in menus or visual references on staff uniforms.

Asian American communities, largely under the auspices of the Media Asian American National Association (MAANA), also organized a protest of Time Warner AOL's decision to broadcast a Charlie Chan film festival. In response to the protests, including petitions and contacting networks, this proposed film festival was canceled. Understanding the varied histories of advocacy strategies might help inform the potential for asserting Arab American voices within cultural production.

Arab communities have attempted to leverage change through organizations affiliated directly with Arab governments as well as through domestic organizations focusing on Arab American constituents. The Saudi government, like many others, employs public relations firms to promote particular images of their communities in the news and other mediated domains; it also bans films such as *The Kingdom*. As Miller and his colleagues explain (2005), governments, such as those in Latin America and western Europe, have been organizing since the 1920s in protest of U.S. film representations of their communities.

While foreign governments may need to be working collaboratively to promote smooth alliances across political administrations, domestic social movement organizations may have more versatility in their repertoires, at times cooperating in order to facilitate political access and at other times resisting and retaliating. The boycott strategy illustrates how the ADC has worked against the media industry in several instances, such as the coordinated movement against the film *Aladdin*. Although this protest was generated on domestic turf, the repercussions spread globally as Arab governments harmonized with ADC's concern about the Disney film.

The ADC's, CAIR's, and others' protest of *The Siege* offers a particularly useful illustration of a mobilization against a film with mixed results. In some senses this protest was successful, in that the news media as well as film reviews recognized the issues raised through the protests and gradually offered more sympathetic coverage (Wilkins and Downing 2002). Yet the film itself was still released, with very few substantive changes made to address concerns with the stereotypical villains.

In his discussion of this particular protest, the film's screenwriter sympathizes with the concerns raised by Arab American groups but tempers this sensitivity with frustration over how he perceives the protests as hurting the film's financial viability. Wright (2004) explains that "this was a hard experience for me, because I completely agreed with the fact that Arabs were stigmatized in Hollywood, and I was very determined not to do that, especially since I had an Arab terrorist in it." He defends the narrative, though, by asserting first that terrorism is realistic, and second, that he included an Arab American character as a heroic FBI agent.

When social movements have the appropriate resources and are able to leverage collective assistance, they do have the potential to move uncontested issues into public discourse. Whether they are able to attract sympathetic media attention may be contingent on their resonance within the cultural context, the particular strategies engaged, and the responsiveness of the media industry. When the media industry seems thoroughly entrenched in its patterns, though, social movement organizations may become frustrated with their inability to influence change, and instead consider alternative approaches to media production.

Working in Parallel to Industry

A third approach to engaging social change encourages the production and distribution of media in parallel with mainstream media industries. How we might understand what constitutes mainstream as opposed to community or alternative media may be contingent on the context of production, but it also draws attention to structural economic arrangements and technological parameters, as well as resonance with dominant ideological themes. First, alternative media might be defined as such in terms of their funding through noncommercial sources, emphasizing the role of these productions as something different from the dominant, larger media industry productions. This notion of alternative might also refer to the types of mediated messages projected, seen as offering some sort of fare divergent from conventional characters and narratives expected through large-scale commercial productions. These conceptualizations of media refer to the economic infrastructure of production and distribution as well as the ideological framing positioning mediated texts in close proximity to political and social elites, emphasizing the value of the alternative in relation to dominant media. Another way to consider this approach would be to downplay this comparison to dominant media industries, instead privileging the role of community participation, understood through particular technological parameters, as part of an assertion of community media (Rodriguez 2001). What one sacrifices in terms of potentially financial viability one might gain in terms of more control over the production of media content.

How media function in terms of their potential to enhance community identity and voice, or even to pose alternative visions, becomes contingent on their political-economic and historical contexts. Given that in the U.S. context, mainstream media production and distribution are governed by the logics of capitalism, through the operations of commercial industries, working in parallel might mean securing funding outside of this profit structure. This potential funding might be composed of public (governmental) and/or nongovernmental sources, which are more concerned with social than fiscal benefit. These possibilities would allow media producers to circumvent the conventional axiom that media products must be commercially viable. Focusing on noncommercial funding builds on an assumption that there is a connection between financial structure and the parameters within which choices are made that result in media content. How to work outside of the corporate structure would be appropriate to consider not only in terms of media production but also in terms of distribution possibilities.

Different technologies offer divergent possibilities for the production and distribution of media texts. If people rely on well-known, prominent television stations, for example, decisions about distribution will be more narrowly centralized through the organizational processes enacted through these bureaucracies. Smaller radio stations, in contrast, might allow more active decision making, thus facilitating community participation. Control over content might also be more manageable through smaller media organizations, whether community television or radio, or even through interactive media such as websites.

While one strategy to promote indigenous voices from nonprivileged communities might engage working within the industry, there are times when working outside mainstream media might help to facilitate this process. Again, the issue of control over content becomes paramount. Various U.S.-based filmmakers, representing a variety of communities outside of the European American nexus, have at times worked through alternative or community-based communication venues. Some film directors cited as having relatively more control over their creative and financial production processes include Robert Rodriguez as well as Spike Lee (Rameriz-Berg 2002). In another example, African American independent film producer Oscar Micheaux distributed his films himself rather than rely on existing commercial channels. This broader movement was designed to create films in which African American actors, directors, and writers would maintain control over media productions, in order to promote narratives through indigenous voices.

In another case, Asian American artists, including film directors, convened to discuss the potential for an Asian American aesthetic, moving toward producing particular films and promoting Asian American actors and directors (Shah 2003). Concerned with stereotypes of "yellow peril," dragon lady, and others, such as more specific antics of Charlie Chan, some Asian American artists pursued alternative means. For example, the Japanese American Sesue Hayakawa, an accomplished actor, initiated a film production company that produced more than twenty films, relying entirely on Asian casts, writers, directors, and other creative artists. A particular cinematic approach, referred to as a triangular cinema philosophy privileging Asian voices in documentary, experimental, and eventually commercial films, emerged through this process. *The Joy Luck Club* represents an integration of this approach into more mainstream Hollywood fare, demonstrating a more financially viable yet potentially less resonant Asian American narrative than that of earlier independent productions. The question of what constitutes an "indigenous" voice remains, given the considerable diversity of backgrounds and positions within any cultural community, and given the recognized processes and structures that reshape whatever goals individual artists might intend.

These strategies have met with varied consequences. At times it is possible to strengthen visions and voices from these communities, yet there remains the potential for co-optation as aesthetics and perspectives become assimilated with dominant characterizations, particularly given the financial risks associated with these projects. And while many notable directors have been able to attract wide critical acclaim, their work has generated controversy as well. Woody Allen, for example, has been noted for engaging controversial topics as well as cultivating broad audiences, offering a complex portrait of a group often marginalized or excluded from mainstream television and film. Provoking debate may be useful in bringing public attention to the underlying issues of representation in connection to prejudice.

Advocacy efforts could benefit from further exploration of the conditions in which individual artists, in connection with and in times in spite of their community affiliations, are able to articulate and control their own narratives. Analyses could assess a variety of these cases, across communities and even across transnational boundaries, given the relative contributions and constraints of national industries (Hollywood, Bollywood, Nollywood, etc.), such as the regulations and policies governing and subsidizing media production, the political ideologies of dominant and resistant groups, the economic structures of production and distribution, and the cultural climates of harassment and intimidation. Similarly, advocacy strategies need to be compared directly, ranging from the more antagonist and controversial to the more conciliatory approaches.

On a systemic level, promoting Arab American perspectives counter to the dominant media portrayals might be advanced through pursuing alternative paths for organized production and distribution. Websites, for example, might help distribute a growing inventory of Arab and Arab American films. Media outlets devoted to Arab American-produced content, such as the Arabic Hour, Arab American News, Arab American Radio Programs, and the Arab Washingtonian, also work through websites to enhance their distribution systems.

Unlike a strategy attempting to inspire emerging creative voices, this approach relies on existing talent and products. Film festivals, such as those promoted through the Arab Film Festival, Mizna, Twin Cities Arab Film Festival, New York Arab and South Asian Film Festival, Seattle Arab and Iranian Film Festival, and the Houston Palestine Film Festival, offer a way to legitimate as well as screen films relevant to Arab American communities. Recently Tony Shalhoub has been supportive of the Network of Arab-American Professionals competition rewarding an Arab American filmmaker, addressing the conference through video in 2004. Rewarding indigenous talent, along with maintaining archives, may help to facilitate the distribution of film, television, and other media offering more sympathetic and complex characterizations of Arab American communities.

REENVISIONING SECURITY AND HOMELAND

Our current media privilege a sense of home within the U.S. territory that reinforces the dominance of European Americans with financial and social capital. Yet we can reenvision our construction of "home" with a more permeable set of boundaries, recognizing that an interest in security needs to consider a variety of concerns both within and outside the territorial boundaries of the state.

This research builds on a comprehensive foundation of literature establishing the limited portrayal of Arab characters and communities in media, illustrating some of the problematic consequences to American audiences. For those identifying with Arab communities, these narratives contribute to concerns with harassment, prejudice, and fear within the United States. For others, keen interest in this genre seems associated with limited knowledge of and prejudicial attitudes toward Arab communities. Media industries assert the limitations of this genre as a way to justify their narrow characterizations and simplistic narratives. While the commercial imperative of the mainstream industry may compel repetition as a less financially risky strategy, enhancing the commercially successful global distribution of action-adventure particularly, there may be room still for creative strategies to incorporate more heroic Arab American characters, positioned within more historically grounded and politically informed contexts.

There is still much more to learn concerning the long-term consequences of mediated Orientalism. Further research on how media portrayals contribute to social prejudice as well as to political decisions needs to build on a variety of methodological approaches, including ethnographic and experimental and survey research, as well as research designs, establishing longitudinal and comparative trends. Corroborating evidence across data sources and methods will help toward establishing evidence that media really do matter.

Finally, more attention to the structures and norms that contribute to the production of these problematic texts may help identify potential leverages for change. Changing media characterizations in this particular instance must also account for the context in which organizations work to promote and reinforce Arab American identity. Collective security in a global context means not antagonizing threatening boundaries, but instead accentuating the humanity and dignity of our rich cultural heritage.

Notes

CHAPTER 1

1. The torture of Arab and Muslim characters in the television show *24* illustrates this dynamic.

2. The latter study by Zelizer and others (2002) points to some interesting distinctions among prominent U.S. newspapers, demonstrating that the U.S. news is not entirely monolithic on this subject.

3. The lack of visibility of the whiteness in central characters is apparent in some scholarly reviews as well. In one example, Lichtenfeld (2004) remarks on a "political correctness in 1990s action films that moves away from foreign villains instead relying on those with "no distinct ethnicity" (171).

4. Thanks to John Encandela for calling my attention to Tonnies's 1887 classic work on gemeinschaft as a more profound and sacred collectivity, as opposed to gesellschaft, as a more utilitarian vision of society in which members belong out of self-interest. Thanks also to Mehdi Semati for encouraging the idea of community based on shared experiences of marginality.

5. This research was supported by a University of Texas Special Research Grant.

CHAPTER 2

6. Jhally and Lewis (1992) also remarked on the way audiences understood clothing as an expression of cultural position, such as the sweaters worn by Bill Cosby on *The Cosby Show*.

7. See Mary Douglas (2002) for exploration of cultural bases for these types of distinctions and attributions. This theme also arises in Shohat and Stam's 1994

discussion of light as part of Enlightenment attention to rationality, juxtaposed with the "dark" of the African continent.

CHAPTER 3

8. These findings resonate with similar projections of East Asian images in film, discussed in Park (forthcoming) and Park and Wilkins (2005).

References

Abou-Alsamh, R. (2007). "Banning 'The Kingdom' Is Counterproductive, Say Experts." *Arab News* (Jeddah), October 12, 9.

Abouchedid, K., and R. Nasser. (2006). "Info-Bias Mechanism and American College Attitudes toward Arabs." *International Studies Perspectives, 7,* 204–12.

Aboul-Ela, H. (2006). "Edward Said's *Out of Place:* Criticism, Polemic, and Arab American Identity." *MELUS,* 31(4), 15–32.

Adnan, M. (1989). "Mass Media and Reporting Islamic affairs." *Media Asia,* 16(2), 63–70.

Ahmed, A. (2002). "Hello, Hollywood: Your Images Affect Muslims Everywhere." *New Perspectives Quarterly (NPQ),* 19(2), 73–75.

Ajrouch, K. J., and A. Jamal. (2007). "Assimilating to a White Identity: The Case of Arab Americans." *International Migration Review,* 41(4), 80–879.

Akram, S. (2002). "The Aftermath of September 11, 2001: The Targeting of Arabs and Muslims in America." *Arab Studies Quarterly,* 24, 61–118.

Alaswad, S. (2000). "Hollywood Shoots the Arabs: The Construction of the Arab in American Culture." PhD diss., Temple Univ.

Ali, K. (2007). "Poetry Can Be Dangerous." *Inside Higher Education.* insidehighered .com/layout/set/print/views/2007/04/23/ali>http://insidehighered.com/la yout/set/print/views/2007/04/23/ali. Accessed April 24, 2007.

Allied Media Corporation. (2006). *Arab American.* www.allied-media.com/Arab-American/default.htm. Accessed April 10, 2006.

American-Arab Anti-Discrimination Committee (ADC) (2003). *Report on Hate Crimes & Discrimination Against Arab Americans: The Post-September 11 Backlash.* Washington, DC: ADC.

Anderson, B. (1995). *Imagined Communities: Reflections on the Origin and Spread of Nationalism.* London: Verso.

93

Amnesty International (2007). *Threat and Humiliation: Racial Profiling, National Security, and Human Rights in the United States.* www.amnestyusa.org/racial_profiling/report/index.html. Accessed March 20, 2007.

Appadurai, A. (1996). *Modernity at Large: Cultural Dimensions of Globalization.* Minneapolis: University of Minnesota Press.

Arab American Institute Foundation (2002). *Quick Facts about Arab Americans.* www.aaiusa.org. Accessed April 10, 2006.

Baker, R. W. (2003). "Screening Islam: Terrorism, American Jihad and the New Islamists." *Arab Studies Quarterly,* 25(1–2), 35–56.

Barker-Plummer, B. (1995). "News as a Political Resource: Media Strategies and Political Identity in the U.S. Women's Movement, 1966–1975." *Critical Studies in Mass Communication,* 12(3), 306–24.

Bateson, G. (1972). *Steps to an Ecology of Mind.* Canada: Chandler Publishing Company.

Brittingham, A., and G. P. de la Cruz. (2005). *We the People of Arab Ancestry in the United States: Census 2000 Special Reports.* U.S. Census Bureau.

Cloud, D. (1992). "The Limits of Interpretation: Ambivalence and the Stereotype in *Spenser: For Hire. Critical Studies in Mass Communication,* 9(4), 311–24.

———. (2004). "To Veil the Threat of Terror: Afghan Women and the Clash of Civilizations in the Imagery of the U.S. War on Terrorism." *Quarterly Journal of Speech,* 90, 285–306.

Condit, C. M. (1989). "The Rhetorical Limits of Polysemy." *Critical Studies in Mass Communication,* 6(2), 103–22.

Dahlgren, P., and S. C. Chakrapani. (1982). "The Third World on TV News: Western Ways of Seeing the 'other.'" In *Television Coverage of International Affairs,* ed. W. C. Adams, 45–63. Norwood, NJ: Ablex.

Daniel, A. (1995). "US Media Coverage of the Intifada and American Public Opinion." In *The U.S. Media and the Middle East: Image and Perception,* ed. Y. Kamalipour, 62–71. Westport, CT: Greenwood Press.

David, G. C. (2007). "The Creation of 'Arab American': Political Activism and Ethnic (Dis)Unity." *Critical Sociology,* 33, 833–62.

De la Cruz, G. P., and A. Brittingham. (2003). *The Arab Population: 2000: Census 2000 Brief.* U.S. Census Bureau.

Deacon, D., M. Pickering, P. Golding, and G. Murdock. (1999). *Researching Communications: A Practical Guide to Methods in Media and Cultural Analysis.* London: Arnold.

Deep, K. (2002). "Deconstructing Hollywood: Negative Stereotyping in Film." *Women in Action,* 3, 57–59.

Dittmer, J. (2005). "Captain America's Empire: Reflections on Identity, Popular Culture, and Post-9/11 Geopolitics." *Annals of the Association of American Geographers,* 95(3), 626–43.

Douglas, M. (2002). *Purity and Danger: An Analysis of Concept of Pollution and Taboo.* New York: Routledge.

Downing, J. D. (2004). "Conference on Re-visioning Arab Communities in US Popular Culture." Presentation, University of Texas, Austin.

Downing, J. D., and M. Beltran. (2002). "The TeleVisions Project: An Exploratory Project on U.S. Entertainment Television and 'Race.'" *Ford Foundation Report.*

Eisele, J. C. (2002). "The Wild East: Deconstructing the Language of Genre in the Hollywood Eastern." *Cinema Journal*, 41(4), 68–94.

Elayan, Y. (2005). "Stereotypes of Arab and Arab-Americans Presented in Hollywood Movies Released During 1994–2000." PhD diss., East Tennessee State Univ.

El-Badry, S. (1994). "The Arab American Market." *American Demographics*, 16(1), 22–30.

EPIC/MRA. (2005). *Survey of Arab Americans*. June 13–22.

First, A. (2002). "The Fluid Nature of Representation: Transformations in the Representation of Arabs in Israeli Television News." *Howard Journal of Communications*, 13(2), 173–91.

Frankenberg, R. (2004). "White Women, Race Matters." In *Oppression, Privilege, & Resistance: Theoretical Perspectives on Racism, Sexism, and Heterosexism*, ed. Heldke, Lisa & O'Connor, Peg, 333–48. Boston: McGraw-Hill.

Gamson, W. (1988). "Political Discourse and Collective Action." *International Social Movement Research*, 1, 219–44.

Ghareeb, E. (ed.). (1983). *Split Vision: The Portrayal of Arabs in the American Media*. Washington, DC: American-Arab Affairs Council.

Gibson, J. W. (1994). *Warrior Dreams: Paramilitary Culture in Post-Vietnam America*. New York: Hill & Wang.

Goodale, G. (2005). "Finally a Film Sheds Muslim Stereotypes." *Christian Science Monitor*, 12.

Gorham, B. W. (2006). "News Media's Relationship with Stereotyping: The Linguistic Intergroup Bias in Response to Crime News." *Journal of Communication*, 56, 289–308.

Grey, H. (2001). "Desiring the Network and Network Desire." *Critical Studies in Mass Communication*, 103–8.

Hall, S. (1985). "Signification, Representation, Ideology: Althusser and the Post-Structuralist Debates." *Critical Studies in Mass Communication*, 2, 91–114.

Hamada, B. I. (2001). "Arab Image in the Minds of Western Image-Makers." International Association for Media and Communication Research Conference (IAMCR), Singapore.

Hanania, R. (1998). "One of the Bad Guys?" *Newsweek*. 132 (18), November 2.

Hicks, N. D. 2002. *Writing the Action-Adventure Film: The Moment of Truth*. Studio City, CA: Michael Weise Productions.

Holmlund, C. (2004). "Europeans in Action." In *Action and Adventure Cinema*, ed. Y. Tasker, 284–96. New York: Routledge.

Howell, S., and A. Shryock. (2003). "Cracking Down on Diaspora: Arab Detroit and America's 'War on Terror.'" *Anthropological Quarterly*, 76(3), 443–62.

Huntington, S. (1996). *The Clash of Civilizations and the Remaking of World Order*. New York: Simon & Schuster.

Jensen, R. (2005). *The Heart of Whiteness: Confronting Race, Racism and White Privilege*. San Francisco: City Lights Books.

Jhally, S., and J. Lewis. (1992). *Enlightened Racism: The Cosby Show Audiences, and the Myth of the American Dream*. Boulder, CO: Westview Press.

Johnson, J. D., M. S. Adams, W. Hall, and L. Ashburn. (1997). "Race, Media, and Violence: Differential Racial Effects of Exposure to Violent News Stories. *Basic and Applied Social Psychology*, 19(1), 81–90.

Kamalipour, Y. (ed.) (1995). *The U.S. Media and the Middle East: Image and Perception*. Westport, CT: Greenwood Press.

Karim, K. H. (2000). *Islamic Peril: Media and Global Violence*. Montreal: Black Rose Books.

Kasem, C. (1990). "Arab Defamation in the Media: Its Consequences and Solutions." *The Link*, 23(5), 6.

Khatib, L. (2004). "The Politics of Space: The Spatial Manifestations of Representing Middle Eastern Politics in American and Egyptian Cinemas. *Visual Communication*, 3(1), 69–90.

King, C. (2000). "Effects of Humorous Heroes and Villains in Violent Action Films." *Journal of Communication*, 50(1), 5–24.

Krämer, P. (1999). "Women First: *Titanic*, Action-Adventure Films, and Hollywood's Female Audience." In *Titanic: Anatomy of a Blockbuster*, eds., K. S. Sandler and G. Studlar, 108–31. Piscataway, NJ: Rutgers University Press.

Kromidas, M. (2004). "Learning War/ Learning Race: Fourth-Grade Students in the Aftermath of September 11th in New York City." *Critique of Anthropology*, 24 (1), 15–33.

Lewis, J., R. Maxwell, and T. Miller. (2002). "9-11." *Television & New Media*, 3(2), 125–31.

Lichtenfeld, E. (2004). *Action Speaks Louder: Violence, spectacle, and the American Action Movie*. Westport, CT: Praeger.

Majaj, L. (2003). "Reel Bad Arabs." *Cineaste*, 28(4), 38–39.

Marchetti, G. (1989). "Action-Adventure as Ideology." In *Cultural Politics in Contemporary America*, eds. I. Angus, and S. Jhally, 182–97. New York: Routledge.

Marrison, J. (2004). "Arabs Not the First to Be Blown Away by the Movies." *Afterimage*, 31(5), 14–18.

Marshall, S. E., and J. G. Read. (2003). "Identity Politics among Arab-American Women." *Social Science Quarterly*, 84(4), 875–91.

Martell, W. C. (2000). *The Secrets of Action Screenwriting*. Studio City, CA: First Strike Productions.

Mask, M. (2004). "Monster Ball." *Film Quarterly*, 58(1), 44–55.

McConnell, H. A. (2003). "The Terror: An Examination of the Emerging Discourse on Terrorism and Its Media Representations." MA thesis, Univ. of Toronto.

Miller, T. (2007). "Global Hollywood 2010." *International Journal of Communication*, 1, 1–4.

Miller, T., N. Govil, J. McMurria, R. Maxwell, and T. Wang. (2005). *Global Hollywood 2*. London: British Film Institute.

Montgomery, K. (1989). *Target Prime-Time: Advocacy Groups and the Struggle over Entertainment Television*. Oxford: Oxford University Press.

Morgan, M., and J. Shanahan. (1997). "Two Decades of Cultivation Research: An Appraisal and Meta-Analysis." In *Communication Yearbook 20*, ed. B. R. Burleson, 1–45. Thousand Oaks, CA: Sage Publications.

Mowlana, H. (1995). "Images and the Crisis of Political Legitimacy." In *The U.S. Media and the Middle East: Image and Perception*, ed. Y. Kamalipour, 3–15. Westport, CT: Greenwood Press.

Muscati, S. A. (2002). "Arab/Muslim 'Otherness': The Role of Racial Constructions in the Gulf War and the Continuing Crisis with Iraq." *Journal of Muslims Minority Affairs*, 1–18.

Naber, N. (2000). "Ambiguous Insiders: An Investigation of Arab American Invisibility." *Ethnic and Racial Studies*, 23(1), 37–61.

———. (2006). "The Rules of Forced Engagement: Race, Gender, and the Culture of Fear among Arab Immigrants in San Francisco Post-9/11." *Cultural Dynamics*, 18(3), 235–67.

Nacos, B. L. (1994). *Terrorism and the Media: From the Iran Hostage Crisis to the World Trade Center Bombing*. New York: Columbia University Press.

Neale, S. (1995). "Questions of Genre." In *Film Genre Reader II*, ed., B. K. Grant, 159–83. Austin: University of Texas Press.

———. (2004). "Action-Adventure as Hollywood Genre." In *Action and Adventure Cinema*, ed., Y. Tasker, 71–83. New York: Routledge.

Negus, K. (1998). "Cultural Production and the Corporation: Musical Genres and the Strategic Management of Creativity in the US Recording Industry." *Media, Culture & Society*, 20, 359–79.

Noakes, J., and K. Wilkins. (2002). "Shifting Frames of the Palestinian Movement." *Media, Culture & Society*, 24(5), 649–71.

Oliver, M. B. (1999). "Caucasian Viewers' Memory of Black and White Criminal Suspects in the News." *Journal of Communication*, 49(3), 46–60.

Omi, M., and H. Winant. (1994). *Racial Formation in the United States: From the 1960s to the 1990s*. 2nd ed. New York: Routledge.

Park, J. (forthcoming). *Yellow Future: Oriental Style in Contemporary Cinema*. Minneapolis: University of Minnesota Press.

Park, J., and K. Wilkins. (2005). "Re-orienting the Orientalist Gaze." *Global Media Journal*, 4(6), Article 2.

Pérez, R. (1985). "The Campaign against Fort Apache—the Bronx." In *Cultures in Contention*, ed. D. Kahn and D. Neumaier, 180–97. Seattle: The Real Comet Press.

Peterson, P. G. (2002). "Public Diplomacy and the War on Terrorism. A Strategy for Reform." *Foreign Affairs*, 81(5), 74–95.

Prince, S. (1992). *Visions of Empire: Political Imagery in Contemporary American Film*. New York: Praeger.

Rameriz-Berg, C. (2002). *Latino Images in Film: Stereotypes, Subversion, Resistance*. Austin: University of Texas Press.

———. (2008). "Manifest Myth-Making: Texas History in the Movies." In *The Persistence of Whiteness: Race and Contemporary Hollywood Cinema*, ed. Daniel Bernardi, 3–27. New York: Routledge.

Rockler, N. R. (2002). "Race, Whiteness, 'Lightness,' and Relevance: African American and European American Interpretations of *Jump Start* and *The Boondocks*." *Critical Studies in Media Communication*, 19(4), 398–418.

Rodriguez, C. (2001). *Fissures in the Mediascape. An International Study of Citizens' Media*. Cresskill, NJ: Hampton Press

Rugh, W. (2004). Senate Foreign Relations Committee Testimony. www.senate.gov/~foreign/testimony/2004/RughTestimony040429.pdf. Accessed June 4, 2008.

Said, E. (1978). *Orientalism*. New York: Pantheon Books.

———. (1997). *Covering Islam: How the Media and the Experts Determine How We See the Rest of the World*. New York: Vintage Books.

Salaita, S. (2005). Ethnic "Identity and Imperative Patriotism: Arab Americans Before and After 9/11." *College Literature*, 32(2), 146–69.

Salame, G. (1993). "Islam and the West." *Foreign Policy*, 2, 22–33.

Salazar, A. (2004). "Arabs in Hollywood: US films' Cultivation of Viewers' Perceptions and Attitudes toward Arabs." MA thesis, Univ. of Texas, El Paso.

Schatz, T. (1995). "The Structural Influence: New Directions in Film Genre Study." In *Film Genre Reader II*, ed. B. K. Grant, 91–101. Austin: University of Texas Press.

Semati, M. (2008). "The Redemption of the Popular: Culture, Difference, and Race in the Age of Empire." Presentation, International Communication Association Conference.

Sensoy, O. (2004). "Popular Knowledge and School Knowledge: The Relationship between Newspaper and Textbook Images of Arabs and Muslims." PhD diss., Univ. of Washington.

Sergent, M. T., P. A. Woods, and W. E. Sedlacek. (1992). "University Student Attitudes toward Arabs: Intervention Implications." *Journal of Multicultural Counseling & Development*, 20(3), 123–31.

Shah, H. (2003). "'Asian Culture' and Asian American Identities in the Television and Film Industries of the United States." *Studies in Media and Information Literacy Education*, 3 (3). www.utpress.utoronto.ca/journal/ejournals/simile. Accessed September 28, 2005.

———. (2004). "Conference on Re-visioning Arab Communities in US Popular Culture." Presentation, University of Texas, Austin.

Shaheen, J. G. (1984). *The TV Arab*. Bowling Green, OH: Bowling Green State University Press.

———. (1997). *Arab and Muslim Stereotyping in American Popular Culture*. Washington, DC: Georgetown University Center for Muslim-Christian Understanding.

———. (2000a). "Hollywood's Muslim Arabs." *The Muslim World*, 90, 22–42.

———. (2000b). "Rules of Engagement: A High-Water Mark in Hollywood Hate Mongering with U.S. Military." *Washington Report on the Middle East Affairs*, 19(5), 15–16.

———. (2001). *Reel Bad Arabs: How Hollywood Vilifies a People*. New York: Olive Branch Press.

———. (2004). "In Its New 'Family Film,' Disney Clobbers Arabs—Again!" *Washington Report on Middle East Affairs*, 23(4), 60–68.

———. (2006). "Arabs and Muslims in Hollywood's *Munich* and *Syriana*." *Washington Report on Middle East Affairs*, 25(2), 73.

———. (2007). "'The Kingdom': Kill 'em All." *The Arab American News*, 23(1130), 15.

Shankman, A. (1978). "Black Pride and Protest:The Amos 'n' Andy Crusade." *Journal of Popular Culture*, 12(2), 236–52.

Shaw, D. (2005). "'You Are Alright, but . . . ': Individual and Collective Representations of Mexicans, Latinos, Anglo-Americans and African-Americans in Steven Soderbergh's *Traffic*." *Quarterly Review of Film and Video*, (22), 211–23.

Sheikh, K. A., V. Price, and H. Oshagan. (1995). "Press Treatment of Islam: What Kind of Picture Do the Media Paint?" *Gazette*, 56, 139–54.

Shohat, E., and R. Stam. (1994). *Unthinking Eurocentrism: Multiculturalism and the Media*. London: Routledge.

Shome, R. (1996). "Race and Popular Cinema: The Rhetorical Strategies of Whiteness in *City of Joy*." *Communication Quarterly*, 44(4), 502–18.

Singhal, A., and E. M. Rogers. (1999). *Entertainment-Education: A Communication Strategy for Social Change*. Mahwah, NJ: Lawrence Erlbaum Associates.

Slade, S. (1980). "The Image of the Arab in America: Analysis of a Poll on American Attitudes." *Middle East Journal*, 143–62.

Solomon, N. (2001). "War Needs Good Public Relations." *Media Beat*. October 25.

Steet, L. (2000). *Veils and Daggers: A Century of National Geographic's Representation of the Arab World*. Philadelphia, PA: Temple University Press.

Suleiman, M. (1988). *The Arabs in the Mind of America*. Battleboro, VT: Amana Books.

———. (2007). "'I Come to Bury Caesar, not to Praise Him': An Assessment of AAUG as an Example of an Activist Arab American Organization." *Arab Studies Quarterly*, 29(3–4), 75–95.

Tehranian, M. (2000). "Islam and the West: Hostage to History?" In *Islam and the West in the Mass Media*, ed. Kai Hafez, 201–18. Creskill, NJ: Hampton Press.

United States Department of State: Bureau of Diplomatic Security. (2003). Political Violence against Americans 2002. www.state.gov/documents/organization/26707.pdf. Accessed April 24, 2007.

Valenti, J. (2002). "Hollywood and the War against Terror." *New Perspectives Quarterly* (NPQ), 19(2), 69–72.

Wilkins, K. (1995). "Middle Eastern Women in Western Eyes: A Study of U.S. Press Photographs of Middle Eastern Women." In *The U.S. Media and the Middle East: Image and Perception*, ed. Y. Kamalipour, 50–61. Westport, CT: Greenwood Press.

Wilkins, K., and J. Downing. (2002). "Mediating Terrorism: Text and Protest in the Interpretation of *The Siege*." *Critical Studies in Media Communication*, 19(4), 419–37.

Wingfield, M., and B. Karaman. (2000). "Arab Stereotypes and American Educators." In *Beyond Heroes and Holidays: A Practical K–12 Anti-Racist, Multicultural Education and Staff Development*, ed. E. Lee, D. Menkart, and M. Okazawa-Rey, 132–36. Washington, DC: Network of Educators on the Americas.

Witteborn, S. (2007). "The Situated Expression of Arab Collective Identities in the United States." *Journal of Communication*, 57, 556–75.

Wolfsfeld, G. (1997). *Media and Political Conflict: News from the Middle East*. London: Cambridge University Press.

Wright, L. (2004). "Conference on Re-visioning Arab communities in US Popular Culture." Presentation, University of Texas, Austin.

Zelizer, B., D. Park, and D. Gudelunas. (2002). How Bias Shapes the News. *Journalism*, 3(3), 283–307.

Index